"There are at least 187 reasons why you should read Herrera's *187 Reasons Mexicanos Can't Cross the Border*. A very abbreviated list would include: because it is some of the strongest poetry, memoir and satire that you will find in one book; because within it are over thirty-five years of artfully recorded passion, anger, engagement, humor and love; because it will carry you across, over and through languages, borders and cultures, revealing truths, asking hard questions and insisting we see the power not only of writer as witness and writer as memory, but the power of writer as conscious revolutionary striving toward a more just and humane world; because it is a pleasure that will awaken and engage all of your senses as it touches and does not let go of your heart."

—devorah major, author of *Brown Glass Windows*, *Open Weave*, *street smarts* and *Where River Meets Ocean*

"Aware, phosphorescent and immediate, this is language brilliantly engaged. Juan Felipe Herrera is simultaneous lighthouse and lightning, the flash that carries the warning and the live wire. For three decades now Herrera's hot-colored Surrealism has transmitted one of the strongest border radio signals of alt-poetics from the Mission District to St. Mark's Poetry Project, from the Taos Poetry Circus to Bisbee, from the first Floricantos of the Bay Area or cross-border exchanges in Tijuana and Mexico, D.F., Chiapas and Yucatán to San Diego, L. A., Austin and beyond. This poetics makes a practice of making a difference. Here available together for the first time are wide-ranging selections from dozens of Herrera's outstanding 'experimental' mixed-genre books, many of which had eccentric or limited original distribution. Contextualized with photos, historical notes and chronology, *187 Reasons* serves up both continental panorama and meta-document in the practice of a poetics that comes alive with startling vitality—across borders of political silence and censorship of the Other, semiotic deserts and actual killing fields."

—Sesshu Foster, author of *Atomik Aztex* and *American Loneliness: Selected Poems*

"Juan Felipe Herrera has written a giant verbal mural bursting with the inventiveness, rhythmic colorings, social engagement and humor—in forms of poetry, litany, and autobiography—that reveal not only the greatness but the absolute necessity of Chicano culture. This is a major generational work by a brilliant practitioner of the art of living the word."

—Jack Hirschman, poet laureate of the
City of San Francisco

"¡Por fin! A manifesto you can dance to. Juan Felipe Herrera's searing laments and soulful riffs don't just electrify. They Mexify."

—Stephanie Elizondo Griest, author of *Around the Bloc: My Life in Moscow, Beijing, and Havana*

"I've been reading Juan Felipe Herrera since he was little baby poet in the 1970s, and this volume, which collects published and unpublished community pieces from the last three decades, gives me an almost painful pleasure. He is the eternal teen poet, the timeless Beat, the premodern postmodern. He is Walt Whitman, Ezekiel, Pablo Neruda, Langston Hughes, Scheherazade, Carlos Fuentes, Allen Ginsberg, Frida Kahlo, Groucho and Karl Marx, Emily Dickinson, Santana, Lao Tzu, and Octavio Paz rolled up and squeezed through dreams of Aztlán and justice and jazz. He is Floricanto. And *187 Reasons*, more than anything he has written, is his autobiography."

—Tom Lutz, author of *Doing Nothing, Crying* and
Cosmopolitan Vistas

187
REASONS MEXICANOS
CAN'T CROSS THE BORDER

UNDOCUMENTS 1971-2007

JUAN FELIPE
HERRERA

CITY **LIGHTS**
SAN FRANCISCO

See page 355 for a list of acknowledgments.

Cover photo by Yolanda M. López
Cover design by em dash
Book design by Gambrinus

Library of Congress Cataloging-in-Publication Data

Herrera, Juan Felipe.
  187 reasons mexicanos can't cross the border : undocuments 1971-2007 / Juan Felipe Herrera.
      p. cm.
  ISBN-13: 978-0-87286-462-7
  ISBN-10: 0-87286-462-6
  1. Experimental poetry. 2. Mexican Americans–Poetry. I. Title. II. Title: One hundred eighty-seven reasons mexicanos can't cross the border.
  PS3558.E74A614 2007
  811'.54–dc22

                                    2007025538

Visit our website: www.citylights.com

CITY LIGHTS BOOKS are published at the City Lights Bookstore, 261 Columbus Avenue, San Francisco, CA 94133.

"Every one of us has to make a commitment to social justice."

—Dolores Huerta

"They say the measure of a good tortilla maker is if you can read a newspaper through it."
—Ofelia Zepeda, "Hot Tortillas," *Ocean Power*

"I believe that everyone is a poet. Everybody is a poet, no one excluded."
—Jack Hirschman, San Francisco Poet Laureate

Grandmother Juanita Martinez de Quintana. El Paso, Texas.
Passport photo, 1934.

For my grandmother, Juanita Martinez de Quintana, my mother, Lucha Quintana Herrera, my father Felipe Emilio Herrera, my second mother, Dolores Robles, my second father, Beto Robles, my second grandmother, Sofía Gonzalez de Oropeza—

pioneers of & for the trail north

For all AB540 students, for my tía Ester Quintana
For Kathy McMahon, Tom Lutz, Jack Hirschman, Genny Lim,
	Francis Wong & Arlene Biala
For Los Manis & Tim Hernandez, David Herrera, Marissa Raigoza,
	Miklos Medrano, Guillermo Gómez-Peña
For Adán Avalos, Kush, QR Hand, Alfonsito Texidor, Jorge Argueta
	& Rubén Martínez
For Victor Martinez, Lauro Flores, Gary Soto & Alejandro Murguía
For Sesshu Foster, Julie Levak, Ralph Lewin & Jim Quay
For Yolanda M. Lopez, John Marron, Ray Gonzalez, Terry Miller &
	Thomas Witt Ellis
For Roberto "Dudie" Alvarez & Karen Hesley
For Victor Carrillo & Ramón García & Roberto Sifuentes
For Emilio Robles Kirkpatrick, Bobby Robles, BJ Robles & Marcos,
	Marisa & Chris Macías
Para todos los poetas fronterizos

For Margarita—
For my children, Joaquín, Marlene, Joshua, Almasol & Robert
For my three teen grandchildren—Jeremiah, Rainsong & Arissa
For Tito, Chente, Chela & Alvina Quintana, Yoli Muñoz & Julian
	Quintana

For Rosita Quintana, RIP

For Carlos Koyokuicatl Cortez, RIP
For Trinidad Sanchez Jr., RIP
For Ricardo Favela, RIP

For José Montoya, Lorna Dee Cervantes, Alurista, Omar Salinas, raulrsalinas, Carmen Tafolla, & Angela de Hoyos—Floricanto pioneers, still blowin' strong

To Benjamin Alíre Sáenz, Daniel Chacón, Victor Hernández-Cruz, Ishmael Reed, Quincy Troupe, Malcolm Margolin, & devorah major

For all Migrant Homelanders sketching a new continent in-between two homelands
For Ferlinghetti & Nancy J, pioneers
For Elaine Katzenberger for bringing this Niñota to light

Om Mani Padme Hum

ACKNOWLEDGMENTS

Gracias to all my publishers through the years—Stephen Kessler, Ernesto Padilla, Nicolas Kanellos, John Marron, Patti Hartmann, Andrea Otañez, Ray Gonzalez, Janet Francendese and Elaine Katzenberger—small press and people's champions who lifted the curtains and set the stage so I and others could say a few words. I thank Elaine Katzenberger twice—for embracing this book with overflowing kindness, art and personal vision. All my poets, dear friends, from San Diego to San Francisco to Seattle, from the East Coast to the Midwest, from Iowa City to New York, from the North to the South, Tijuana, Mexico City and beyond, you have brought me here, with your voices, magazines, friendships and hearts. To all the teatros, cafés, neighborhood bookstores, bilingual radio stations, self-made poetry circles, tiny art galleries and hometown libraries—this is because of you. Gracias to all the schools, community centers, poetry places, universities and city and community colleges across the United States for inviting me to put a word in the air, a good word for the belly and the soul. Thanks to Paola Castro, Mayra Ortega and Ngoc Luu for countless hours and two years of going through nine books and various broadsides and transcribing texts for this collection. I thank my Huichol and Maya families that welcomed me into their houses made of tree, earth, rock and redwood, thank you for your generosity, stories, life, vision and silences—*pampayusi*. And again—gracias del corazón to Mrs. Lucille Sampson from third grade, Logan Heights, San Diego, for shocking me saying I had a beautiful voice, for Mr. Daniel Hayden in sixth grade in San Francisco, for urging me to tackle theatre, and Mr. Harrison-Maxwell, at San Diego High, for warning me that I was still only using one-third of my voice in choir. And my students, through the years, I bow to you, you have sharpened my work and nourished my life-path. There are no words to express my gratitude to my soul-partner, Margarita Robles, for her wise counsel, and my children and grandchildren, for their lives, laughs and patience. Papá Felipe was the one that took my family on daring voyages with nothing but a few pesos in the pocket; his campesino choices made the earth come alive. My mother, Lucha Quintana, was the first one to show me, day after day, the art of the heart, and how to paint, dance and sing with it. And you standing here—let the the good words—*las buenas palabras*—for peace and justice roll.

TABULA RAZA

AVISO  FOREWARNED

Juan wrote in a frenzy. Poems and antipoems—antipoems most of all.
He was fixed on tearing the new language out of the old structures.
—from "The Third Conversation," *Mayan Drifter*

The lines of type on the following pages may at first glance resemble poetry or prose, but if you look and listen closely you'll find they are more like footprints: tracks in which can be heard the rhythms of migrating feet—running feet, trudging feet, marching feet, dancing feet—feet on the move propelled by their own momentum. You may also hear the sounds of wheels, wheels of Mustangs and Volkswagen Bugs, Chevy pickups and Mexican buses, wheels of trains and minivans carrying faces and voices across landscapes, across personal and cultural geographies, across public and private terrain where history, in all its distance and intimacy, can't be kept from happening.

Juan Felipe Herrera's writings are charged with theatrical and athletic energies, with the excitement of extemporaneous performance, spontaneous invention and rebellion, the claiming of physical and psychic territory, the thrill of discovering natural reserves of resilience and creativity—the resources to live, as Emerson called them—powers of insurgent improvisation. Gathered from more than thirty-five years of work in various genres, these "undocuments" are the record of an epic journey across many different borders, frontiers, wildlands of transformation, boundaries of nations, state lines, city limits, edges of farmland, roads through rain forests, urban curbs along nostalgic streets of dreams and nightmares, heterodox crossings and impure mixtures of languages and literary forms, dramatic forms, forms of oratory and investigation, the lyric and the documentary, memoir and satire, incantation and exhortation, autobiography and social history, the pamphlet, the broadside, the joke—inwardness, outwardness, in-betweenness.

A sustained manifesto of resistance and affirmation, political protest literature untainted by self-righteousness, its rhetoric subverted by self-questioning, its anger tempered by tenderness, its comic riffs seasoned with tragic understanding and its tragic laments lightened by laughter, Herrera's writings have the courage of range, the restlessness of a mobile imagination that dares to leap through its doubts into deeper doubts, which give way to a rock-solid confidence in its destiny as a medium of individual and collective expression.

From the campos of Mexico to the campuses of California, the deserts of the Southwest to the pre-silicon city of San José, the barrio of East L.A. to the bohemia of Venice West, the urban labyrinth of Mexico City to La Misión of San Francisco, from Fresno to Chiapas, San Diego to Tijuana and back, with foxlike zigzags and formative stays in acutely recalled neighborhoods, alternate roots reaching every which way to anchor the drifter in specific kitchens, dragging the shadows of hotels and the heat of fields where his parents labored and afforded him the adaptive vision and versatility to fashion a different scenario for himself, Herrera remembers everything and gives back to his native places and to the family, friends and compañeros of his Mexican/American/Chicano odyssey a scrapbook, a logbook, a journal, a multiform confession of proud hybridity and indigenous optimism.

Papers? Permits? Documents? Identification? Open this file anywhere and find the authorization to keep on, permission to be who you are in your own skin, license to cultivate your inner guerrilla, angelic visas of transcendent transit. This book is the passport to a country under construction. It is a symphony for cyclone fence and hundreds of miles of breezes that swirl right through, raising clouds of aroused music. The world you are entering is one where idioms mix promiscuously and the earth itself can be heard speaking several tongues through the soles of your surprised feet. Listen to the footsteps echoing in the footprints and be moved.

—Stephen Kessler

Tía Lela and Mamá Lucha Quintana. Niño Perdido, Mexico City, D.F., circa 1918. Zinc plate.

FLORICANTO SALUTE

In xochitl, in cuicatl.

In this collection I have gathered my performance & text-in-the-community work—which is at the core of all Chican@ poetry, in particular, my cadre, the Floricanto generation of '71, probably ignited by Alurista's publication of *Floricanto* & José Montoya's *El Sol y Los de Abajo*, Bernice Zamora & Antonio Burciaga's *Restless Serpents*, Chican@ Latin@ theatre, poetry and arts marauders and books of Chican@ and Latin@ poetry for the people. Along with the word-throwers, the Chican@ small press publishers of the Southwest fueled the early out-loud word—such as *El Grito del Norte* from New Mexico, Lorna Dee Cervantes's *Mango Press* in San José, the Bay Area's *Tin-Tan* and *El Grito* from Berkeley. In the midst of these journals we had the periódico movement, people's papers from *La Verdad* in San Diego, *El Tecolote* in San Francisco to the hundreds of other little papers mostly across the Southwest as well as those in Mexico and Latinoamérica—fused with community art, song, news and word. César Chávez's pioneering United Farmworker campesino newspaper, *El Malcriado,* featured alabanzas (sacred song-poems) and corridos and mostly ran its course through the small towns and camps of the California valleys. We were editors-poets-designers-publishers-and-distributors. And the word? Well, it was spoken in all forms and across time and space—*La Prensa*, from San Antonio, was perhaps the first brave periodical in Spanish that focused on the political and cultural experience of the Mexican and Latin@ migrant homelanders during the years of the Mexican revolution. We were inspired by these forerunners. As the sixties ended, a Canto Wave appeared: The first annual Floricanto Chicano Literary Festival, held November 13–14, 1973, at the University of Southern California. This was the initial challenge for an organized national Chican@ & Latin@ canto community, founded by Alurista in 1973. From those two days forward, we recognized our faces and rekindled our voices. And we traveled together, wrote together and organized together. To this day, with the energy and heart of many groups, the Floricanto poetry movement and converging literary communities continue to transform and expand through tributaries flowing across the nation, Mexico, Latin America, Europe and Asia.

Here, in this tribute to the Floricanto movement, the pieces are laid out as if they were speaking in their community–moment in time, when their gestation was in motion, and in most cases when their environments and/or narratives were formed; these years are indicated at the beginning of each chapter. Their actual publication sources and dates appear at the bottom of the texts. At times, I have added an "Aztlán Chronicle," people-news of a sort, to give the sections and the book a little more topography, context, micro-historical sense and mostly a Floricanto sound—& a saludo to the manifold communities of word & soul. I bow to all the home-grown journals, community silk-screeners, small-pressers adjacent to delis & donut shops, chapbookers in flats & apartments, newpapers cut & pasted with hot-wax irons in garages, and Floricanto-word pioneers that have passed on, such as the great mimeographer-poet Corky Gonzalez, postcard & muralist poet Antonio Burciaga, borderlands language-conjurer Gloria Anzaldúa, and Motown word-caller Trinidad Sánchez Jr. among many other beautiful women and men—Floricanto singers.

May the *canto* of and for the people flourish in its multiple forms, like the mini-painting-poem handouts Jack Hirschman gives away on the streets of San Francisco and in the "New Media" electric pages of the Net-Roots blogger & on-liner movement. As a dear friend, Alfonsito Texidor, one of the Prime Ministers of the Word in San Francisco's Mission District, says, "Get on down to the coffee grounds. . . ."

I didn't start out to be a poet. Because I had been silenced, I started out to be a speaker.

Juan Felipe
Redlands, TierrasRojas, Califas, September 2007

"Their powers shook them. They vibrated, they thundered and the stars came out of their mouths."

— Perfecto Segundo, Cahuilla shaman, telling the creation story of how Mukat and Témayawet spoke out the universe from their hearts. Early 1900s. As transcribed by Katherine Saubel, Cahuilla elder. From *Inlandia*, Heyday Books. 2006.

Their Powers Shook Them

AZTLÁN CHRONICLES, VOL. 1, NO. 9

Out I jumped as we had for decades ecstatic electric bit-
tersweet clown with Cantínflas long slow-slung pants flat
beaten shoes & shredded seersucker shirts among the ambling
lines of Mexican kids half-way between being Mexicanos &
the other half about to mutate into Chican@hood about '68,
with Roman campesino eyes & Centeotl-Catholic dresses &
bow-legged kicks at the free-speech mound rallies & huelgas
sit-ins love-ins & be-ins screaming then hissing then voice
cracklin' hauling back all the memory & blowing wide all
about the new prisms & jazz crazy keys of our neo-nation
Aztlánamérica that tenuous & fuzzy diamond child crashing
out of our goofy out-of-hock talkative harmony mouth address-
ing the blank space of time we were there somewhere in this
new voice-light still standing dodging & boxing back the
onslaughts of the '50s, '60s, & later the 187s the 227s the
border "operations" immigration sweeps on the way to school
the deportations in the middle of a dream all those bad-nasty
tawdry numbers plans ideas policing-policies apropos micro-
apartheids those slick matter-of-fact Saturday-nite racisms
bannered & finally bandaged by other soon-to-be de-throned
terms & actions against history & people's true freedom

187 REASONS MEXICANOS CAN'T CROSS THE BORDER

circa 1992-2006

In 1940, activist Luisa Moreno was asked to speak before the American Committee for the Protection of the Foreign Born. Her speech, which became known as the "Caravan of Sorrow" speech, eloquently described the lives of migrant Mexican workers. Portions of it were reprinted in the Committee's pamphlets, creating a legacy that lasted much longer than the duration of the speech itself. In it, she stated,

> *These people are not aliens. They have contributed their endurance, sacrifices, youth and labor to the Southwest. Indirectly, they have paid more taxes than all the stockholders of California's industrialized agriculture, the sugar companies and the large cotton interests that operate or have operated with the labor of Mexican workers.*

187 REASONS MEXICANOS CAN'T CROSS THE BORDER
(remix)

—Abutebaris modo subjunctivo denuo.

Because Lou Dobbs has been misusing the subjunctive again
Because our suitcases are made with biodegradable maguey fibers
Because we still resemble La Malinche
Because multiplication is our favorite sport
Because we'll dig a tunnel to Seattle
Because Mexico needs us to keep the peso from sinking
Because the Berlin Wall is on the way through Veracruz
Because we just learned we are Huichol
Because someone made our IDs out of corn
Because our border thirst is insatiable
Because we're on peyote & Coca-Cola & Banamex
Because it's Indian land stolen from our mothers
Because we're too emotional when it comes to our mothers
Because we've been doing it for over five hundred years already
Because it's too easy to say "I am from here"
Because Latin American petrochemical juice flows first
Because what would we do in El Norte
Because Nahuatl, Mayan & Chicano will spread to Canada
Because Zedillo & Salinas & Fox are still on vacation
Because the World Bank needs our abuelita's account
Because the CIA trains better with brown targets

Because our accent is unable to hide U.S. colonialism
Because what will the Hispanik MBAs do
Because our voice resembles La Llorona's
Because we are still voting
Because the North is really South
Because we can read about it in an ethnic prison
Because Frida beat us to it
Because U.S. & European Corporations would rather visit us first
Because environmental U.S. industrial pollution suits our color
Because of a new form of Overnight Mayan Anarchy
Because there are enough farmworkers in California already
Because we're meant to usher a postmodern gloom into Mexico
Because Nabisco, Exxon, & Union Carbide gave us Mal de Ojo
Because every nacho chip can morph into a Mexican Wrestler
Because it's better to be rootless, unconscious, & rapeable
Because we're destined to have the "Go Back to Mexico" Blues
Because of Pancho Villa's hidden treasure in Chihuahua
Because of Bogart's hidden treasure in the Sierra Madre
Because we need more murals honoring our Indian Past
Because we are really dark French Creoles in a Cantínflas costume
Because of this Aztec reflex to sacrifice ourselves
Because we couldn't clean up hurricane Katrina
Because of this Spanish penchant to be polite and aggressive
Because we had a vision of Sor Juana in drag
Because we smell of tamales soaked in Tequila
Because we got hooked listening to Indian Jazz in Chiapas
Because we're still waiting to be cosmic
Because our passport says we're out of date
Because our organ donor got lost in a Bingo game
Because we got to learn English first & get in line & pay a little fee

Because we're understanding & appreciative of our Capitalist neighbors

Because our 500-year penance was not severe enough

Because we're still running from La Migra

Because we're still kissing the Pope's hand

Because we're still practicing to be Franciscan priests

Because they told us to sit & meditate & chant "Nosotros los Pobres"

Because of the word "Revolución" & the words "Viva Zapata"

Because we rely more on brujas than lawyers

Because we never finished our Ph.D. in Total United Service

Because our identity got mixed up with passion

Because we have visions instead of televisions

Because our huaraches are made with Goodyear & Uniroyal

Because the pesticides on our skin are still glowing

Because it's too easy to say "American Citizen" in cholo

Because you can't shrink-wrap enchiladas

Because a Spy in Spanish sounds too much like "Es Pie" in English

Because our comadres are an International Political Party

Because we believe in The Big Chingazo Theory of the Universe

Because we're still holding our breath in the Presidential Palace in
    Mexico City

Because every Mexican is a Living Theatre of Rebellion

Because Hollywood needs its subject matter in proper folkloric
    costume

Because the Grammys & iTunes are finally out in Spanish

Because the Right is writing an epic poem of apology for our proper
    edification

Because the Alamo really is pronounced "Alamadre"

Because the Mayan concept of zero means "U.S. Out of Mexico"

Because the oldest ceiba in Yucatán is prophetic

Because England is making plans

Because we can have Nicaragua, Honduras & Panama anyway

Because 125 million Mexicans can be wrong

Because we'll smuggle an earthquake into New York

Because we'll organize like the Vietnamese in San José

Because we'll organize like the Mixtecos in Fresno

Because East L.A. is sinking

Because the Christian Coalition doesn't cater at César Chávez Parque

Because you can't make mace out of beans

Because the computers can't pronounce our names

Because the National Border Police are addicted to us

Because Africa will follow

Because we're still dressed in black rebozos

Because we might sing a corrido at any moment

Because our land grants are still up for grabs

Because our tattoos are indecipherable

Because people are hanging milagros on the 2,000 miles of border
    wire

Because we're locked into Magical Realism

Because Mexican dependence is a form of higher learning

Because making chilaquiles leads to plastic explosives

Because a simple Spanish Fly can mutate into a raging Bird Flu

Because we eat too many carbohydrates

Because we gave enough blood at the Smithfield Inc., slaughterhouse
    in Tar Heel, North Carolina

Because a quinceañera will ruin the concept of American virginity

Because huevos rancheros are now being served at Taco Bell as
    Wavoritos

Because every Mexican grito undermines English intonation

Because the President has a Mexican maid

Because the Vice President has a Mexican maid

Because it's Rosa López's fault O. J. Simpson was guilty
Because Banda music will take over the White House
Because Aztec sexual aberrations are still in practice
Because our starvation & squalor isn't as glamorous as Somalia's
Because agribusiness will whack us anyway
Because the information superhighway is not for Chevys & Impalas
Because white men are paranoid of Frida's mustache
Because the term "mariachi" comes from the word "cucarachi"
Because picking grapes is not a British tradition
Because they are still showing *Zoot Suit* in prisons
Because Richie Valens is alive in West Liberty, Iowa
Because ? & the Mysterians cried 97 tears not 96
Because Hoosgow, Riata and Rodeo are Juzgado, Riata and Rodeo
Because Jackson Hole, Wyoming, will blow as soon as we hit
    Oceanside
Because U.S. narco-business needs us in Nogales
Because the term "Mexican" comes from "Mexicanto"
Because Mexican queers crossed already
Because Mexican lesbians wear Ben Davis pants & sombreros de
    palma to work
Because VFW halls aren't built to serve cabeza con tripas
Because the National Guard are going international
Because we still bury our feria in the backyard
Because we don't have international broncas for profit
Because we are in love with our sister Rigoberta Menchú
Because California is on the verge of becoming California
Because the PRI is a family affair
Because we may start a television series called *No Chingues Conmigo*
Because we are too sweet & obedient & confused & (still) full of rage
Because the CIA needs us in a Third World State of mind

Because brown is the color of the future
Because we turned Welfare into El Huero Félix
Because we know what the Jews have been through
Because we know what the Blacks have been through
Because the Irish became the San Patricio Corps at the Battle of
    Churubusco
Because of our taste for Yiddish gospel raps & tardeadas & salsa
    limericks
Because El Sistema Nos La Pela
Because you can take the boy outta Mexico but not outta the Boycott
Because the Truckers, Arkies and Okies enjoy our telenovelas
Because we'd rather shop at the flea market than Macy's
Because pan dulce feels sexual, especially conchas & the elotes
Because we'll xerox tamales in order to survive
Because we'll export salsa to Russia & call it "Pikushki"
Because cilantro aromas follow us wherever we go
Because we'll unionize & sing *De Colores*
Because A Day Without a Mexican is a day away
Because we're in touch with our Boricua camaradas
Because we are the continental majority
Because we'll build a sweat lodge in front of Bank of America
Because we should wait for further instructions from Televisa
Because 125 million Mexicanos are potential Chicanos
Because we'll take over the Organic Foods business with a molcajete
Because 2,000 miles of maquiladoras want to promote us
Because the next Olympics will commemorate the Mexico City
    massacre of 1968
Because there is an Aztec temple beneath our Nopales
Because we know how to pronounce all the Japanese corporations
Because the Comadre network is more accurate than CNN

Because the Death Squads are having a hard time with Caló
Because the mayor of San Diego likes salsa medium-picante
Because the Navy, Army, Marines like us topless in Tijuana
Because when we see red, white & blue we just see red
Because when we see the numbers 187 we still see red
Because we need to pay a little extra fee to the Border
Because Mexican Human Rights sounds too Mexican
Because Chrysler is putting out a lowrider
Because they found a lost Chicano tribe in Utah
Because harina white flour bag suits don't cut it at graduation
Because we'll switch from AT&T & MCI to Y-que, y-que
Because our hand signs aren't registered
Because Freddy Fender wasn't Baldomar Huerta's real name
Because "lotto" is another Chicano word for "pronto"
Because we won't nationalize a State of Immigrant Paranoia
Because the depression of the '30s was our fault
Because "xenophobia" is a politically correct term
Because we shoulda learned from the Chinese Exclusion Act of 1882
Because we shoulda listened to the Federal Immigration Laws of
        1917, '21, '24 & '30
Because we lack a Nordic/Teutonic approach
Because Executive Order 9066 of 1942 shudda had us too
Because Operation Wetback took care of us in the '50s
Because Operation Clean Sweep picked up the loose ends in the '70s
Because one more operation will finish us off anyway
Because you can't deport 12 million migrantes in a Greyhound bus
Because we got this thing about walking out of everything
Because we have a heart that sings rancheras and feet that polka

187 Reasons Why Mexicanos Can't Cross the Border, 1994. Revised.

21 RATIONAL REASONS REPUBLICANS CAN'T JUMP

Because they are burning down posters advertising churros on sale at
Wal-Mart
Because they are busy banning Spanish from public plazas and
people's places
Because their pockets are still lined with old right-wing lobby nickel
Because they are chained to their property in Rancho Mirage
Because their property is really our property in Rancho Mirage
Because jumping reminds them of crossing La Border
Because their shoes got shined in Tijuana on Avenida Revolución
Because they are kneeling down praying for things to stay the same
Because getting way too high is not the proper way of doing business
Because they are staying low searching for WMDs
Because they are waiting for instructions from Lou Dobbs
Because Lou Dobbs can't jump
Because they are chasing La Migra to speed things up a bit
Because they are chasing La Policía to speed things up a bit
Because they are hanging out with developers building another
super-max prison
Because Dolores Huerta didn't hand them a towel
Because wearing Tommy Hilfiger loafers & Perry Ellis bathrobes
drags you down
Because the word *change* can easily turn into a *chinga*

Because they are carrying the red states by a hair
Because the word Republican comes from the word Republicant
Because whenever they look up they see an alien about to land on
    them

New work

MEXICAN
DIFFERENCES
MEXICAN
SIMILARITIES

You build the fence we climb the fence

You hammer it up we rock it down

You draw the line we erase the line

You reinforce it we loosen it

You block it we dig under it

You use nightvision we use huaraches

You use bomb-smelling dogs we use chorizo-scented cucarachas

You ask Are you an American Citizen? We say Yes way before you

You organize we unionize

You chew tobacco we chew cacti

You call on the governor we call on each other

You speak in English we speak in between what you speak

You say oyster we say órale

You say tomato we say salsa

You say potato we say papas

You eat lettuce we irrigate lettuce

You eat grapes we pick grapes

You decorate Xmas trees we farm Xmas trees

You eat turkey on Thanksgiving Day we raise the turkeys for
     Thanksgiving Day

You sit at the table we serve the table

You dance on the floors we mop the floors

You sleep in hotel beds we make the hotel beds
You've got the law on your side we got history on ours
You get the message this is the message
You build border walls by the minute
Every minute we cross a thousand

You play baseball we play baseball
You watch Oprah we watch Oprah
You shop at Costco we shop at Costco
You burn under the sun we burn under the sun
You call this place California we call this place California
You have a family we have a familia
You watch *General Hospital* we watch *General Hospital*
You speak a little Spanish we speak a little Spanish
You read the *NY Times* we read the *NY Times*
You grab a cab to a George Lopez show we grab a cab to a George
    Lopez show
You love the eggrolls at the deli we love the eggrolls at the deli
You listen to New Age music we listen to New Age music
You gotta problem with terrorism we gotta problem with terrorism
You wonder about the President we wonder about the President
You want more rights we want more rights
You stroll the Golden Gate we stroll the Golden Gate
You read Stephen King we read Stephen King
You climb Half Dome we climb Half Dome
You lost someone in the war we lost someone in the war
You download Alica Keyes we download Alicia Keyes
You wonder about the universe we wonder about the universe
You wheel grandmother to the home we wheel grandmother to the
    home

You ride the BART to nowhere we ride the BART to nowhere

You can't quite put your finger on our similarities
We can't quite put our finger on our similarities

New work

HOW TO MAKE WORLD UNITY SALSA

For Ray González, George Kalamaras, & Thomas W. Ellis.

Mash the pulp
Mash the pulp
Mash the pulp
Add a burned tomato & a rock of garlic
Add a burned tomato & a rock of garlic
Mash the pulp
In the black stone bowl
Mash the pulp
In the black stone bowl
Put your hand into it
Put your wrist into it
Put your shoulders into it
Mash the pulp in the black stone bowl
Mash the pulp in the black stone bowl
Put your hips into it
Put your hips into it
Char another chile
Char another chile
Mash the pulp
In the molcajete
Mash the pulp
In the molcajete
Just a pinch of salt

Just a pinch of salt
Pour the soup from the tomato heart
Pour the soup from the tomato heart
Now throw your head back twice
Now throw your head back twice
Mash the pulp in the molcajete
Mash the pulp in the molcajete
Mash the pulp in the molcajete
Yellow chile
Red chile
Green chile
Black chile
Brown chile wrinkled
White garlic
Black chile
Green chile
Red chile
Brown chile wrinkled
Yellow chile
Now throw your head back twice
Now throw your head back twice
Breathe baby
Breathe baby
Breathe baby
Breathe baby
Your fingers on the rock
Your palm on the stone
Your eyes on the inside
Your bones on the soul

From *Notebooks of a Chile Verde Smuggler*, 2004.

Riverside Train West

AZTLÁN CHRONICLES, VOL. 1, NO. 1

Uproar of music from the rail coming my way standing a few
yards from the 91 heading east west in the center of river-
side town gray & pounding light downtown like all my
downtowns desolate & confetti-like antique stores & mis-
sionization ghosts in the lost hotels & smoky libraries
museums & clean flower-colored skiddly-boom windows for
tourists & homeless woman draggin her plastic multi-col-
ored bags May springtime a block from university avenue
where chicano town eastside dwells with a panadería here &
there tire shops a barbería & more hotels slumped to one
side searching for shade & emptiness some call it progress
that old '50's concept we all saw on the first-time TV
black & white some folk saw it color so the train rolls
sweet bent & stops & I take my ticket & camera bag & grab
a seat coming from san bernardino banging bullet rails &
six dudes in loose white T's & blues shaved clean heads
plump bellies from the cabbage potato & starch jail lunch
sit & lean & jump up & hang & jive in their pathos in the
clanging train car moving now honking now heading to LA I
sit & slip a tiny paper pad from my hip pocket & scratch a
few hook lines been living in redlands teaching at UCR
figure I'd come back to so-cal where I kicked off in '56
childboy from ramona mountain east of san diego life sad-
happy from traveling in papa felipe's jaunty troka dodge
army grilled san joaquín valley days of picking grapes &
living in trailers on the side of old dusty towns ham sand-
wiches in greyhound diners & yellowish cafeterias on the
road subtleties the train rumbles fulfilling its mission
en route to Los where the Day Without a Mexican march is
bubbling with life & lives helicopters cops old movimiento

hipsters new generation post-colonial smarties & farm
worker straw voices & feet stomping so I sit back a little
& we halt in corona where twelve almost falling on their
face mexicanos climb in wearing the code dress of white
T's like me & the jailbird dudes on the side on another
track home they roll in wearing miniature americano flags
& holding day-glo posters as if checking out of a kinder-
garten crafts workshop this train this train I breathe in
& out I bow & notice this is a freedom train going west
more mexicanos more stops a mexican freedom train two chi-
canos wearing laker shirts & untouched eyes their bodies
in trance too I ask them stuff jot it down next to the aged
black man who says what's going on like marvin gaye says
what's going on we tell him all about the march the ille-
gal rap the undocumented rap the alien game language trip
we been dealing with for years generations & lives almost
as gorgeous as the stars old man laughs cool & says I was
there I been there you know what's going on it's all about
throwing you in prison 'cause you don't have papers about
making you a felony-man a felony-woman in the cage like I
was I served my time lemme tell you I been there I was
there first time I saw a hummer was in victorville when I
was in prison there we were putting the hummer together &
we fixed up the wiring harness for the cobra helicopter in
that facility got paid pennies per hour boy that's what
it's about I been there we sent food to desert storm when
I was at Boron Kramer Junction by highway 38 three years I
did we made everything you know mattresses pillows PJs
pants shirts khakis for the federal system in atlanta some
guys got sent to lompoc some to oklahoma city some to
pueblo colorado it ain't fair that's what they wanna do to
you I see what they're doing they take you to El Reno
detention center free labor free labor that's what it's
all about it's freeze-cold in the hills in Boron we made
axles & coil springs we ate chicken in a pan chicken &
dumplins then he says Mel's my name he says you all paid
your dues your ancestors paid your dues you don't owe
nothin' they owe you yeah you'd be surprised the biggest

crook wins then nothing happens then Mel gets off near LA
I don't know what to say he's sayin' it sounds like all
prison-speak sounds something that makes sense when you
are on the inside too long too easy to make sense the young
chicanos ask me if I am a journalist with my notes & cam-
era no I say just going to the city where we got a day

A DAY WITHOUT A MEXICAN

May 1st, 2006

Continue the Struggle in Anthony's Name. L.A. City Hall, May 1st, 2006.

Our Chicana Lady of Justicia on Broadway. L.A. City Hall, May 1st, 2006

A DAY WITHOUT
A MEXICAN
VIDEO CLIP

Mass demonstration,
May 1st, 2006, L.A. City Hall

For Anthony Soltero, April 24, 1991–March 30, 2006. RIP.
For the Corrales family.

The march is holy
      we walk we   float up

the hill from Broadway from
      Spring Street from Union Station
from Main to City Hall without leaders

everyone everyone   alone is a leader   woven
      everyone is   here

      between exile and homeland
          an exile without a name or a territory
             a homeland that does not   exist

      we walk that is all

at the center from all four directions red

Che Guevara flags white
T's & jogger pants baby blue red & white
against the ancient trees crossed

arms open dangling hearts

the eyes above below blonde & black

you have never seen this we have never seen this brown &

concrete shadow a buzzed head tiny boy with plastic

tattoo
Mexican
flags

on his cheeks & on the arm where the watch goes

where time is absent up
another flag & a pair of binoculars swing

swing

around his tender neck he is serious he is

searching

roll rolling the red & white & blue flag whose flag

his flag
whose flag
behind him a sign cut out
in black against white on the street

    "We are Americans" can you read it from there

       can you hear it
can you feel it down below the earth   mouth mother
Coatlicue of the serpent skirt down   down
below
Xibalba chambers of the dead centuries stolen lands occupied

    all this comes back
    a man with black glasses steps by

    below the hill bicycle man
    dressed in Uncle Sam
track shoes & backpack drenched

    red & white & you again

    the flag against the red the blue against the white again
    the whirr in the center   the void the vortex

    unanswered questions
    the obedience of the street alone
riding the wheels
      gazing up another man   strums the guitar

remember Víctor Jara remember Chunky Sanchez
remember the two million lines
from a César Chávez corrido
sung across the rose-worker
          MacFarland fields of '64

bow to the honey-colored woman

in yellow with baby in orange shirt her face Cimabue

      would paint the building behind us tilts
      forward falls toward the sign "Muchos inmigrantes más mejor"

      "The more immigrants the better" what

      is an immigrant that is the question
      what is a migrant that is the question

      what is a homeland that is
      the question each face

has a question today a homeland
each face has an answer   today
how will   you read this when a chavalo
      holds up a red flag
      in camouflage jungle suit black beanie Mexican flag

52

wrapped around his face Subcomandante Marcos style
Chiapas style Indian style revolution style

today we are   the style

for the day
for the next Congressional Hearing
can you hear this? play the guitar my brother

bar the chord the F then the B
then the G minor a shaved Chicano
& a chavala 16 years old long dark tresses

set against the white light blaze blast
another Chicana sits on the curb

with her sign

"Humans not aliens humanos no marcianos" red

smeared into black feet shuffle

behind her all directions at the same   time

can you see her from there
can you read her from here
who is reading

53

read read read read
up high mid-level

where the horizon trembles   a Danzante de la Conquista
in warrior stance with la Virgen de Guadalupe estandarte
cradle strapped behind his back 4 feet high

sonaja rattles
in silver-plumed motorcycle glasses

 waves the Mexican flag feathered too
at the edges frayed the march

from Mexico City Plaza Tlatelolco Plaza Zócalo conchero danzante
still in rebellion against   Spanish rule still

following the first danzantes migrantes pioneers
in soul danza Andrés Segura Granados &
          his arrival

          Toltecas en Aztlán
          Centro Cultural de la Raza
occupied water tank summer of '73
          San Diego leader of the Xinachtli danza clan Colonia Obrera D.F.
          warrior & history visions across the States

followed in '74 by Florencio Yescas Guerrero danzante pioneer
with clan Esplendor Azteca Colonia Roma
stomp your feet

stomp your heart stomp
the cement & circle

blurred figures in flames
it was Cerillo whirling thin drumming Teponaxtli tall it was
Piolín jive talking Colonia Tacuba style it was Conejo always sayin'
"lesgo" instead of "let's go" it was Lázaro keeper of the incensario &
copal it was the fire burning against the skin in the center of the plaza
it was me in the shape of a whisper flame in Taos High assembly hall

San Diego again Floricanto festival again in Austin Texas when
Tomás Atencio invited us to Peñasco danza at the hall late night Taos
Pueblo to bow before Blue Mountain sacred earth grandmothers
danza danza under choppers & bodies woven spiritual

everyone marches & doesn't   notice
a woman ambles by me golden & indigo

pulls at her sign "Hoy marchamos mañana votamos" "today we march
tomorrow we vote" who will vote is   the question

where will we vote is   the question
in what gerrymandered Republican neighborhood
I lost the question

a four-year-old on his dad's shoulders
Spiderman cap his father in military camouflage hat

zoom right to the fifty-seven porta-potties

sixty Chicanos stand sit lean over the plastic domes
with horns & Mexican flag Superman capes &

more hats & more signs &
more cardboard & more marker scribble
"Es mejor vivir luchando que vivir humillado toda la vida"
"It is better to live fighting than to live humiliated all your life"

this is the tone
this is the tenor this is the   song
"Todos contra el muro" "All against the border wall"

a grandmother cherubic María cherubic Rita
cherubic carries a baby with a Buddha hand

blessing the way
parting the waves a Chicana streaked blonde
hair pulled back checks her cell phone cut
to "Viva México" jump-cut to "Son of Pancho Villa Warrior" a scene
from Teatro Campesino 1971
with Smiley Rojas playing the role of Cantinchuko

& Teatro Rayos de Quetzalcoatl 1973
          Son of Pancho Villa smokes a cigarette
white bicycle cruiser white shoes spotless black glasses
spotless he smokes with one hand in his pocket another

Chicana ruby lips tangerine jeans & a friendship bracelet sits at
the curb touches her poster in the human

flow flow flow flow flow flow day-glo green
against her breast "The world can't wait to drive out the Bush
regime—amnistía general" she sits

& notes a vato with a South Pole T & a baby held up
in the sky further up

lonesome smog technocrat needle City Hall monolith
cut to a flowering tree blossoming
unknowingly

without advance notice eight teen Chican@s
in between its amber liquid branches with flags & signs & flags

& hats & caps & Cruz Azul & denim pants
one muchacho is on fire inside I can tell by the face
the color brown going into a reddish flare igniting igniting

in this collective soul awakening he reminds me
of the boy last scene of *Los Olvidados* by Buñuel dumped

at the edge of Mexico City DF

down the waste pile
dead anonymous
this is his reincarnation   now

rise above all of us &

 cut to the freeway overpass
             more flags & lines of gente

             flagging 18-wheelers

honk & Honda Civics cut to 2 Chicanas with Zapatista kerchiefs
 & black shades Señorita Revolución Señorita Frida reborn

Chicana Chinas Poblanas reclaim the revolution
what revolution
what Frida

a new term unread   a new prophecy uncut
& not yet fully uttered cut   to everyone is here

the past becomes the present where we march
& the future appears in beige glimpse snaps

     flows webs   legs torsos astute & falling forward & blood
the flavor of watermelons & murmuring

"Continue the struggle in Anthony's name" teen Chicano from De Anza Middle School Ontario California 12 miles west of Riverside Anthony Soltero now gone

to the skywaves 4/24/91 to 3/30/2006 suicide after being warned & reprimanded for participating in a walkout for migrante justice

      Anthony may you rest in peace
      this is for you
this
is for   you

      cut to the left a teen Chicano
      below Anthony's sign meditates grows older glistens darkens

      under the solar orb a 14-year-old girl caresses the sign
        next to Anthony's mother Anthony looks this way

      white T blue backdrop he gazes alive
      almost   he is
Here Now

      a Chicana with a ten-gallon hardshell hat blonde
      aside two kids balances towering flags cast shadows

      on the sidewalk in the shape of a tear
      & a bomb profile in black slow slung
      & a chekere shake shakes African beads

white nylon
umbrella with glitter gold lettering
"Justicia para todos" the figures flow

into each other after   centuries & cities   cut in half
a chavalo with a starry cape a chavala
with the eyes & color of a Huichol sorceress a mara'akame
rests her chin on a red stripe &

another performero

Uncle Sam man about 16 yrs old poses & lifts one arm for a photo
   shoot

   à la Anthony Quinn
   reminds me of my nephew Junior Melendez
   in Mesa Arizona working for Southwest Airlines
   with his sad angry eyes high up

   by the helicopter sound & bellies & legs wrinkled &
   two men under a sales tent "Stolen Lands"

   T in black solid for sale walk on
   walk on everyone walks on with torn islands

of ice in their hands cell phones & water bottles &
a guitar strums "Tuvimos muchos señores unos fueron tigres
otros fueron leones" the song Jorge Luján taught me in 1985

& a Chicano friar dressed

in blue-black tunic stands
by the overpass hands me scapularies
who will save us

who will save him

is there still room for America to be saved ? hands me a can
for change with the figure of el Santo Niño de Atocha

little omchild holy in a colonial dress of angelic powders
the boy my mother Lucha led me to at Guadalupe church in
        Logan Heights, San Diego, 1958

play play another guitar brother
in EZLN shirt &
long hair pluck the chord ecstatic

determined holy Indian eyes dark face skin
with flame torch hair "We are not criminals" the sign reads
        a city of signs a language of signs   a nation

in formation announces its credo

another guitar stands against the fire hydrant

by itself walking by itself for itself
"We know it is racial" another banner under

wet humid trees pinned in between
the chord sounds   jump-cut to a three-year-old & lollipop

"Yo nací en América soy Americano ok" Chicano atop
the porta-potty flies his banner over the thousands
another leans on a tree above the rest
"A Day Without a Mexican" two carnales

show off their T's a chavala 17
bites her apple in between the bodies rising

the speaker talks about power
then static light comes down hard from the sky
can't tell it if it is light or

sound
human
or chopper machine blades &
a chavalo beats a drumstick
against his own hand
to feel if he is here this side

that side this side
that side walk walk walk play strum save all of us
save that guitar in black & white & yellow in shade

in shorts guitar made of walking

nothing has changed
everything is walking
moving flowing blending seeing falling rising being

marching dissolving Chicano 14-yr-old
across the treetops where he climbs as if
he found a ladder to the 13 heavens of Omeyocán

Che Guevara T red & black he peers out
into the multitude for the first time 800,000, 600,000 500,000
he meditates from there he stops   the world from there

he notices the universe

the flow of jelly wire hearts the blood
churns the light burns this reading skin

unveiled
he gazes out first time affirmed
unknown unclassifiable vortex of soul spirit family clan mi-
grante

nation crossers nation makers

flow flow flow two men & a woman jog down dark
under the sheet they hold over their heads I stop

under
for a moment my father Felipe appears
for a second underneath the campesino tarp
Lake Wolfer 1954
east of San Diego mountains we eat soft sweet flour tortillas

from the woman comal at the center cinnamon
dirt hard worker arms after dusk

we gather alone drink eat speak caress
the green air we gasp it is possible at times
to bring everything together &
through the human sleeve a new society

for a minute or two a birth again

human face heart body electric sweat breath
breathe breathe papa Felipe holds me come alive
again face to face nothing changes

only everything three Chicana teens sit on a concrete banister
two smoke one reads news in a yoga position

city hall yellowish CNN trucks unravel cables

thousand eyes international
we chant below
　　　we chant above

　　　　a grandmother sits on the curb
　　　for a minute & lets her grandchild
　　　pet her black and white doggy

　　　in blue straps she wears Indian porcupine needle earrings
　　　a hard carnal with red bandanna throws words

　　　into his tight microphone words against colonialism
　　　words against multinationals words big words
revolution words his chuko tando hat pulled low
he keeps talking we keep marching

　　　　the tide takes us
we fall & fly & go & roll & walk
& swing & fuse "We are America" the boy rolls up his flag

we chant in the circle
　　　sacred sign the shrine in paper
　　　& poster paint facing the earth

now
a skull shield

warrior races down the street alone
as if no one is here he races

with pheasant feather headdress & penacho breastplate
beaded gold burnt sienna burnt black faceless
he runs where are the others where where is America

where is this city where are we walking ?

a teen Chicana with a Teotihuacan T & a grandmother lean
  into each other by a tree leg bandanna & a rebozo crimson

        gaze across the throngs across the Chicano Moratorium of '70,
August 29
        is that where you gaze where Rubén Salazar dissolved

        with a gas canister at the Silver Dollar bar where
        thousands marched for the moratorium against the Viet Nam war

        where some died shot down
        here on the marching streets where
        is the news crew

where is the CNN truck the cables grandmother eyes grand-
mother eyes on migrantes

across two homelands Mexican@ latinoamérica
birth death

usa two planets
two selves two voices
two tremors
two nations
two breaths
two trees
two into one

into the black made of shadow & fire
one of stone one of water one of void
one of fullness breathing at the same time
migrant homelanders & carnales & carnalas
climb on asphalt some on sidewalks
some in trees some on hills some on bicycles

some alone some in groups some still
on porta-potty roofs some dressed

as Mexican superheroes
flags across shoulders flags as skirts
& hats & tattoos & cheeks in performance
& paint Van Goghs on poster board

for citizenship after centuries of labor
a Chicana with a Harley shirt & bongos strapped to her belt
beats the skins
     bebop
     bebop bebop
     bop bop pop pop

     be be be be blam a breathe

     explodes the multitude
     a Chicana with a white Santa Claus scarf black marker across
her cheeks the face of Cuauhtémoc the face Siqueiros painted

     Cuauhtémoc-woman bare breasts & hands
       scratching out the canvas you say is art or a poem or a text
           that cannot be summarized or framed into flames
only flames

     read it

       she writes on her face "unity"
writes on her face "unity" her sister carnala
in rainbow rebozo
 wrapped around her shoulder points up

a young mother & baby sways

to the rhythms
all of our bodies a vato pulls off his shirt tattoos

on his back jagged strokes metallic tokes
angles broken stars & leaning letters flesh fences
busted across his shoulders saunters

return to Anthony Soltero's mother
stands in white T brilliant with a foto
pressed on her chest with Anthony
as a child boy she looks hard at all of us

as we rise up
her eyes diamond then soft into
this new marching first time
all walking together flow flowflowflow

flow

New work

Che Migrante, "A Day Without a Mexican." Mass demonstrations, City Hall Park, Los Angeles, May 1st, 2006.

On Vulture Road

AZTLÁN CHRONICLES, VOL. 1, NO. 2

Go down to Juárez once in a while then see my grandmother's
grave in El Paso Paisano Drive Evergreen Cemetary right
across Chico's Tacos a ways down where you can order round
hot dogs colored carmine red Juárez the town Dylan sang
about with his sawdust voice with an offbeat twang that
town where my mother Lucha came in the early 1900s scrap-
ing a life toward El Norte years later making it to the big
time El Paso Texas Overland Street the buttery gate where
Pancho Villa & Anthony Quinn's mother almost met in those
stumbling wow change days splashed on the streets & soft
adobe brick walls blown by fire tempered desert winds
orphaned from the jagged spirit peaks warring in the yin
yang between two nations one made of geometry & ambition
the other of fanged mountains & desire now combined in this
maquila town Juárez chipped by smoke & wiry harsh torsos
so many women young ones murdered en route to the big cry
norte joy this town of bullet-riddled knife-riddled gov-
ernment-riddled man-riddled usurpations colonias that
endure one or two rains one or two waves of mayors & prom-
ises & PRI posters & glamorous shoe stores & fallen powdery
murals of Hidalgo in the Nowhere sad brown openscapes of
the poor beat pit life if you have wings if you can fly
manically up there by those shredded clouds you look down
for a second or two with ant eyes with skinny-bone squir-
rel eyes & you will feel the shape of this town skin
offspring of the two counter-nations this revolution town
this town of our exploded merciful futures in the sleek
contour of a vulture may it become an eagle again

SEÑORITA X
SONG FOR THE YELLOW-ROBED GIRL FROM JUÁREZ

Circa 1990–2006

Juárez collage by Karla R. Garzón-Zárate. Fresno, 2004.

SEÑORITA X
Song for the Yellow-Robed Girl from Juárez

Yellow-robed girl
Yellow book schoolgirl
Yellow horn-rimmed glasses gazing girl
Yellow purse yellow sigh maquila girl woman
Yellow time in between fire and desire girl
Yellow norte-bound solitary lonesome working hard woman girl
Yellow painted hands in the night shuffling home girl
Painted by the moon only
Guided by the moon only
Advised by the moon's dry sorrowful heart woman
Yellow-robed girl robed in desert dust arrow light

This is your song
This is your song
This is your song

To remember you
To locate you
To defend you

This is the song of mourning mothers with revolution guitars

This is the song of mumbling fathers with harmonicas conjuring the
    winds
This is the song of tiny lost brothers and sisters hiding under
    mercado glass
This is the song of dead uncles and dead aunts still in search for you

This is the song of grandmothers and grandfathers calling you from
    the mountain crest
This is the song flying in all directions where everthing lives where
    you live

This is the power song you gave me
An old woman corn harvest song

An El Paso hollering tortilla vendor song
A Juárez marching black thriftstore and miracle powder street bruja
    song

Listen
Yellow-robed girl woman:

The border aching raining lies
The border rain tearing leaves trembling with more lies and curses

From a hut speckled with weed aluminum cigarette coffeecan life
From an unending crime scene spilled disturbed jostled and jimmied
From the winds come down from Cristo Rey Mountain where we
    climb on our knees
From Anapra Town below below way below where you

Lived for three weeks en route to Anthony en route to Mesquite en
   route to Los Angeles

You
Buried beneath twenty years of killings
You
Yellow-robed girl lacking the breath now full spirit
You
Raise yourself from the rock cross dust edge of Juárez

Bring back your mind from the station wagon dumpster hole
Bring back your eyes from the death dirt whip cut knife whirl
Bring back your body from the formless sex destruction sites
Bring back your voices the ones you left curled by the asphalt
Bring back your tender broken hands bring them back to wholeness

You were dressed to work at Zapatería Tres Hermanos you laughed
You were planning to review your résumé at the maquila office #7
You were filling out an application for the Tecnológico de Monterey
You were biting your lips then rewriting your poems yours

Brown
Thin
Young
Thin Brown
Young thin
Young
You
Were without an age
You were without weight

You were without color
Someone took you
He saw the age
He measured your body
He counted your short years

6
7
8
9
10
11
12
13
14
15
16
17
18
19
In between
Below and above in between below and above above below

A man
Un hombre
An older man
Un hombre mayor
A staff man a man in charge
Un chófer a driver a technical man
Un señor un policía un hombre de categoría

Un simpático un educado un animal peinado de hombre
A man with a group of man friends associates managers
A man with a map a set of directions orders investigators questions
Un abismo de drogas en chaketa en voz en manos brazos gruesos
    truenos
A man in charge of the room and the sales position you applied for
Ese hombre de corbata de lengua de palabras de filos de sangres

This is your song:

Hijas de Juárez
Hijas de México
Hijas de Centro América
Hijas de Chihuahua
Hijas de Zacatecas
Hijas de Nayarit
Hijas de Michoacán
Hijas de Oaxaca
Hijas de Sonora
Hijas de Sinaloa
Hijas de El Paso
Hijas de América

    Who's the killer Brenda Berenice Delgado?
    Who's the killer Alma Chavira?
    Who's the killer Verónica Martínez Hernández?
    Who's the killer Esmeralda Herrera Monreal?
    Who's the killer Mayra Reyes Solís?
    Who's the killer Guadalupe Luna De La Rosa?
    Who's the killer Griselda Mares?

Who's the killer Silvia Elena Rivera?
Who's the killer Olga Alicia Carrillo?

Here lies
The coroner's office tiny flat table chrome a hacksaw a hammer a
string
Here lies
The maquila dressing room tilted oblong wet walls the floor
spotted set for rape
Here lies
The police report trapezoid open at the beginning at the end
closed stuffed erased
Here lies
The bus tire track the chófer the steering wheel the tires the
gasoline all in agreement to kill
Here lies
The shoe sales shop main street downtown the employer the
window case the shoes stained
Here lies
The investigator federal prosecutor the state agents the drug
haulers the official story
Here lies
The road midnight in between the moon and the knife the
feathery breath you

Here lies
The mountain above you
        jagged jaw mandible broken pilgrimage mountain
        miniature replicas of saints along the way waiting praying
frozen melting

Here lies
more paperwork scribbled with a make-believe name
not your name a make-believe name you

Listen:
¿Almaalambre brendabranded lupelost gloriaboneaglow
irmamopped mayramadthenight
Guadalupefromwhere mariaycllownow aracelionly6 welosthername
heroriginalname?
This report has been filed in accordance with the proper policy for
identifying the dead

Who's the killer Brenda Berenice Delgado?
Who's the killer Alma Chavira?
Who's the killer Verónica Martínez Hernández?
Who's the killer Esmeralda Herrera Monreal?
Who's the killer Mayra Reyes Solís?
Who's the killer Guadalupe Luna De La Rosa?
Who's the killer Griselda Mares?
Who's the killer Silvia Elena Rivera?
Who's the killer Olga Alicia Carrillo?

Lissen again:

The mothers walk the mountain edge with a mysterious sign
The mothers float over Juárez in long ragged dresses of fire
The mothers weep and organize the mothers all the mothers
The mothers move across the desert and the cities they move
The mothers carry banners & paints & photographs & naked lights

The mothers rip open the earth with their mouths open open
The mothers flesh out the darkness and beat it with their electric eyes
The mothers walk in hunger forever hunger forever ancient hunger
The mothers swing hammers against the walls & columns of smoke
The mothers wear red-sequined shawls in pieces flying to the skies
The mothers break windows and stairways & city hall watchtowers
The mothers charge radios & antennas & satellites on their heads
The mothers bake clay and make offerings of little girl flame figures
The mothers drain the river el Río Bravo the snake blade in green
    wounds
The mothers sew with their long fingers the daughter hair back into
    the earth
The mothers pull pull the earth lips and press press the blood singing
The mothers gather the blood mounds the blood cakes the blood
    cups
The mothers push the blood ocean & cradle close the blood crib cry
The mothers paint their faces with the daughter blood and daughter
    moon glow

Listen:

The mothers are not mothers anymore
They are the black center where you dwell
They are the churn howl creation where you rise again

Yellow-robed girl

New work

400 Murdered. ZERO Convictions. INFINITE Loss.
Who will speak for our Mother's, Sister's and Daughter's?

"Remember Juárez," by Anthony Cody, Fresno, 2004.

Doublenation-Doubleheaded Warriors

AZTLÁN CHRONICLES, VOL.3, NO. 3

"We walk to find our lives..."

— Ramón Medina Silva, Huichol Shaman, Double-Nation Ambassador, 1971. RIP

Jammin' home down Interstate 10 through Palm Desert late
April after the Tomás Rivera Conference Floricanto #34
after listening to Jesús Martínez Saldaña speak. on
migrantes from Michoacan it all dawns on me—migrantes
rebuilding Mexico fountains city parks primary schools &
businesses back in the hometown, sending cash & new strate-
gies back to el pueblo & back to here: mobilizing marching
political-walking out of schools & jobs for justice for
citizenship organizing into local committees centros
gazettes & wires blogs & websites panaderías & barberías
supermercados & abogados. The migrante is the new double-
headed warrior like the sacred Eagle Girl maíz deity of the
Huichol—*Tatei Werika Wimari*—a double-headed eagle she
refashions borders she nurtures a new polity stitched with
the last scraps of the ancient corn societies—stands up
this fluid double-nation wingspan eagle flare of libertad

ONE BY ONE
Circa 2004-2008

For José Fernando Pedraza-Estrada,
a day-laborer, killed in Rancho Cucamonga, California,
by an out-of-control car, while marching
against current immigration policies.
May 6, 2007

ONE BY ONE

For Jorge Argueta from El Salvador and
Mayra and Alfonsito Guillén from Arizona who
lived and related these stories and for all desert-warriors.
For the owl & panther children poets of Tucson, Arizona.
For Carlos Fuentes.

One by one
two by two they galloped
across the clouds and the flowers
across black corn fields
and exhausted sands
one husband
one woman
two
fourteen-year-olds
one
with a blue straw gunnysack
another
with a bag of lemons and hard bread
barefoot with bedsheets knotted into eights
to dream of rivers driven into one
to raise the arms toward the sky
to sleep
open-air
on the wooden slate and
the numbers of the night
violet thorns
and tiger storms and

tigers without tongues
it was mayra it was alfonsito
it was grandmother doña soria from atizapán
two and one
three and two one and
no one even though they had
names like lalo and lupe
and pepe and araceli names
without letters or stars
better yet
they were no one
said the wind
no one
said the river
you are like me
said the yellow-green water
you are transparent fleeting you rise and fall
appear and dissolve among the others
like you
like me
like no thing
like water
for a moment
there was silence
there was a breathing in the desert
of winds and souls aflame
they boarded a bus
one by one
busload of sheet metal and cardboard
hopes and resentments

from leaving themselves behind
their clouds and their forests
two by two
almost
dressed up made up
socks of sand shoes made of rubber
and inside the girdles and belts
folded pesos
tiny green and scarlet
and blue-yellow bills turned
into miniature trumpets
a roll of yesterday and tomorrow another
twisted into knots without victory
without dreams without a throat
only the little voices
from that ranchito
sobbed in the distance
that pueblito
of shadow ashes and
candles color of copper and sun
why are you here from where
how many remain
how far you headed paisana
they spoke like this
on the rough sands
sure of their triumph and that paradise
norteamérica
that is how they scattered under
the black trees that is how they gave sweat
in the train cars color of brick

color of oil and fog
that is how they were left
under the silvery leaves
it is the moon that calls us
hey moony moon they said
give me a flask of your water white fresh
hey moonmoonymoon
sang the children give me
a pony made of rainbows and
white gold blankets
so we can find the river where
no one will see us hiding doubled up
one by one
this is how their dreams arrived
walking
dragging themselves hugging each other
through the tunnels the canyons this is how they lived
inside tarps and sad holes and fiesta cloth and
newspapers and movie posters of the famous
without sun without earth or house without anything
no sky nor floor
they were twenty they were eight
fifteen one
then two
they were infinite
they could taste it
in the bread they felt it
in the murmur
of the branches and
the barrack's riddled wall

señor coyote's
almost time
almost the hour almost late this very minute I'll take you
he told them at the hour when all cats are grey at night
and he smiled and they handed him two thousand from their bags
and they gave him a tip and they offered him
three thousand each one each two
stay here
I'll be right back to pick you up
that's what señor coyote told the eleven-year-old boy
from santa tecla from that forgotten volcano
that was his promise to the girl from san pedro guatemala
and they gave him all they carried in their jute bag
and they emptied their kerchiefs on the wet sand
and they were left naked
on the tin sheets trembling
one by one two by two
washing up their hands preparing
and wetting their braids
once again they waited
for the morning light of daybreak
with more dreams of the states
with more dreams of their mother
the mother
whips clothes against the water-well stone
in the pueblo of kindling wood slivers the kind
that flourishes in springtime
the kind that almost smells of honey
when you burn it
in the thick night

go now
it's time here take this
everything I have one day we'll meet again
one day you'll see we will all be together
step into the bus son
step in my little girl do not cry now
do not think about this that is what the mother said
wringing her hands
blessing them on the corner
that rectangle of nothingness
that bone oven
this is how they dreamed the mother
on the corner
short and poor
with dead eyes and her voice
at three in the morning every second whirred
waiting for señor coyote
señor coyote in his station wagon mirrors and exhaust
with his watch and his mustache and
his hair the shape of fire
we have known many señores
they whispered to each other
some were tigers
some lions others wild boar some howler monkeys
what more can we do
and they waited shivering in between wood slats
one by one
against the wall of the abyss
that cage of voices and eyes on fire
salvadoran some whimpered guatemalan others

shouted chiapas man veracruz tabasco michoacán
this is how their voices twittered each one
as if they had nations
as if they had lands
as if they had countries
so many voices fell on those crazy windows
that smoke without carbon
he never arrived
señor coyote the coyote señor was
below the tin sheets and cylinders he was
celebrating with beers and mariachi hits
at the table he was
with his guys his hometown boys
he hovered in the tiny circus of that pueblo
on the mountains towering over nothingness
tasting tacos filets leg meat brains
tripe breaded steak gizzard and chicken
shoulder bone smoked sausage and pork rind
he was laughing with his mouth full of corn
and his oiled cowboy shirt the color of roses
one by one two by two
they escaped
one by one
two by two
you jorge
you margarita
you vicente and florencio
you alma and esperanza
a wife a young man alone
with swollen eyes

with sores on the lips
the throat shut tight the legs
without a planet or a season
it was summer it was always time to pick produce
it was summer eternal incandescent time
without time to return as giants
to go back south one day
this is how they drifted
one by one
two by two
they were fourteen they were six
without water
without bread
without a name
without licenses
without papers
without a wallet
without stars
a busload of shadows and nightriders
some dragged underneath
some behind
others further below
others in the trunk
others with shoulder blades against the engine
charring their skin
burning and screaming
melting down drop by drop
arm by arm
but no one heard them
no one

had a clue
only the wheels tearing
only the chrome filaments of the metals
grating the asphalt toward the north country
only the night jungle
made of wires giraffes rifles jewels
one by one
two by two
you maría
and juana and norma and teresa
you francisco apolonio fernando roberto
they huddled onto another bus
we are almost there brother
see we can do it little sister
this is how they spoke half asleep
half dead and buried
they stopped at a checkpoint
and the soldiers spoke
where are you from boy
tell me what pueblo
the green-suits asked
I am a mexican
I am a mexican
I am a mexican
one by one they said
then two
by two
they were twenty-five
they were fourteen
I know where you are from

and where you are headed get down
or I will get you down
and that is how they fell
with their shredded skirts
with their huaraches and
string shoes
and they threw them in jail
some made calls
others
stayed fallen without breath
some were taken
by brothers or an aunt
the rest knelt on the dirt battered
with eyes lacking water
grey cold and their hands
swollen hard fifteen years old
twenty nineteen fifty-six like this
alone in those broken skeletons take off
the blouse pull down the underpants
let's see what you have there
and no one found out
and no one
said a word
drinking café con leche
in the offices no one
searched for them
the others took off running
it was a lottery night without reimbursement
it was a desert that never ended
and they cried among themselves

I am free at last
at last I am headed to the states
I want to make some dollars
a few greenbacks for
my mother and my children and
a chevrolet pick-up but not a new one and
they darted toward the lights
yellow and red and blue and white
like fire and alarms in that salt
ice and flame at the same time
then those lights switched off
there were more patrols more soldiers
and they jailed them
behind bars again
one by one
two by two
they were so numerous they seemed
like the desert itself
busted black the color of smoke
and the waves of voices and blood rushed
each night only this held them
the crevice of landscape a fan of weeping
that abyss where they were born
without a name without a memory
only a faraway heat
the nothingness echo they suffered
some slipped out could barely see
others stayed under the shadows
and there they drowned in the sea of iron cells
one by one

two by two
they were thirty
they were five
they were eternal a husband
one wanted to be a student
wanted books to study
wanted to sport a blue accountant suit
one wanted a household
another wanted to learn english
one by one
they opened the desert
it resembled méxico
without jaguar skin
guatemala without
lakes or volcanoes
it resembled puerto libertad
but without water or an oar
it resembled janitzio but without blue green
one by one they crossed
two by two
miguela eleven years old
maría dolores garcía lópez quintana carrillo
and more names like martínez álvarez garza avina
monreal sifuentes smith corona a husband
a young one a boy
lost searching for his mother another
turned upward and noticed white carnations
they are rain clouds they are the words of god
it is a ship of shadows this is how they spoke when
they crossed the red sands

by the tumbleweeds
until they landed
on the Tohono O'odham reservation
miles from agua prieta naco
and beyond tucson
until they dissolved
among the shacks
government sponsored shrunken
by the blue fire of the heavens
some stayed behind digging
scratching the earth
tastes like rain
tastes like milk
and there they closed the eyes
the eyelashes popped stiff
forever
others
hid themselves
in the tin-sided indian houses they robbed
they broke the beds and the tin cases and nothing
they found in the small ribbon boxes
only ash and more shadow more sand
nothing and everything
one by one they followed
the road to no place toward
a dream without earth without horizon
their lips lost their hands cut
their hearts only their hearts
were left but they were not hearts anymore
they were empty of blood

and rhythms of breath
it was an ancient tree
that tore out of the chest
a soul
of orange-colored branches and lavender nests
torn without honeyed water only leaves
thorns bones shadows fires
then the earth opened made of dry lights
and more patrols and more cells and more ovens
one by one
two by two
I am alive
or I am dreaming
I am dead they spoke like this
those figures
crossing
deserts across deserts
notice the flowers and the rivers
the thin rain and fountains and chickens and town feasts
the gardens the sky clean the casas ours the
dishes of pastries and jellies and salsas and beans and
little gifts and the horse from the ranchito
and the water-well brimming and the laughter maría and pedro
and josé and marianito maruch
saying hello one by one
two by two they arrived caressing
their children and their weary dogs
destroying burning the horizon little roads and bitten fields
when they lived in another time in another life
like this they arrived where they began

one by one
two by two
their mouths
stung by bees
their hands as if almost playing guitars
crossed over the breast
in a box without a name
in between dry wood slats
the color of wine color of never always
wrapped in foreign sheets
    their lips half open as if about to drink water
    their hair thin brilliant waving
        in the winds

New work

UNO POR UNO

Para Jorge Argueta de El Salvador y
Mayra y Alfonsito Guillén de Arizona quienes
vivieron y me contaron estas historias, y
para todos los cruzadesiertos.
Para el grupo de niños y jóvenes poetas,
buho y pantera de Tucson, Arizona.
Para Carlos Fuentes.

Uno por uno
dos por dos cabalgaron
a través de las nubes y las flores
a través de las milpas negras
y arenas desganadas
un esposo
una mujer
dos
de catorce años
uno
con mochila de tule azul
otro
con un saco de limones y pan duro
descalzos con sábanas hechas ocho
para soñar los ríos hechos uno
para alzar los brazos hacia el cielo
para dormir
abiertos
en la tabla y los números de la noche
espinas violetas

y tigres tiniebla y
tigres sin lengua
vino mayra vino alfonsito
vino la abuelita doña soria de atizapán
dos y uno
tres y dos uno y
ninguno aunque tenían
nombres como lalo y lupe
y pepe y araceli nombres
sin letras ni estrellas
mejor aun
no eran nadie
decía el viento
nadie
decía el río
eres como yo
dijo el agua amarillaverde
eres transparente fugaz subes y bajas
apareces y te desvaneces entre los otros
como tú
como yo
como nada
como agua
por un momento
hubo silencio
hubo un respiro en el desierto
de vientos de almas en llamas
en un camión se montaron
uno por uno
al camión cargado de láminas y cartones

esperanzas y
resentimientos
de alejarse de sí mismo
de sus nubes y sus bosques
dos por dos
casi
vestidos casi arreglados
calcetines de arena zapatos de hule
y en los cinturones y fajas
pesos doblados
pequeños verdes y guindas
y azul amarillo billetes hechos
trompeta en miniatura
un rollo de ayer y mañana otro
hecho nudo sin victorias
sin sueños sin garganta
sólo las vocecitas
de aquel ranchito
lloraban de lejos
ese pueblito
de sombras cenizas y
velas color de cobre y sol
para qué vienes desde donde
cuantos quedan
hasta donde le das paisana
así platicaron
en las arenas toscas
seguros de su triunfo y aquel paraíso
norteamérica
así corrieron bajo

los árboles negros así sudaron
en los trenes color ladrillo
color aceite y niebla
así quedaron
bajo las hojas plateadas
es la luna que nos llama
oye lunitalunera dijeron
dame un vaso de tu agua blanca fresca
oye luna lunita lunera
cantaron los niños dame
un caballito de arco iris y
zarapes blancos de oro
para alcanzar los ríos donde
nadie nos ve escondidos trenzados
uno por uno
así soñaron
caminando
arrastrándose abrazándose
por los túneles las barrancas así vivieron
en carpas y hoyos secos tristes y pañuelos de fiesta y
periódicos y carteles de cine de los famosos
sin sol sin tierra ni casa sin nada
ni cielo ni suelo
eran veinte eran ocho
quince eran uno
luego dos
eran infinitos
lo probaban
en el pan lo sentían
en el murmullo

de las ramas y
en el paredón del cuartel
del señor coyote
ya casi
es hora casi tarde ahorita los llevo
les dijo a la hora cuando todos los gatos son pardos
así les sonrió y le dieron dos mil de su bolsa
y le dieron una propina y le ofrecieron
tres mil cada uno cada dos
quédate aquí
luego vengo a recogerte
así le dijo el señor coyote al muchacho de once
desde santa tecla desde un volcán olvidado
así le prometió a la niña de san pedro guatemala
y le dieron todo lo que traían en sus mochilas
y vaciaron sus paliacates en la arena mojada
y se quedaron desnudos
en las láminas temblando
uno por uno dos por dos
lavándose las manos preparándose
y empapándose las trenzas
esperaron una vez más
la luz de la quebrada
con más sueños de los estados
con más sueños de su madre
la madre
azota ropa contra la piedra del pozo
en aquel pueblo de astillas de ocotillo del que
florece en las primaveras
del que huele casi como la miel

cuando lo quemas

bajo la noche espesa

vete ya

es hora ten te doy

todo lo que tengo un día nos volveremos a encontrar

un día ya verás todos estaremos juntos

súbete al camión hijo

súbete hijita ya no llores

no te preocupes así les dijo su madre

torciéndose los dedos

bendiciéndolos en la esquina

ese cuadrilátero de la nada

ese horno de huesos

así soñaban todavía a su madre

en la esquina

chaparra y pobre

con ojos de sepulcro y su voz

a las tres de la mañana cada segundo giraba

esperando al señor coyote

al señor en su camioneta de espejos y rehiletes

con su reloj y su bigote y

su pelo hecho fuego

tuvimos muchos señores

se decían

unos eran tigres

unos leones otros jabalíes unos saraguatos

que más podemos hacer

y los esperaron titiritando entre las rendijas

uno por uno

contra la pared de abismos

esa jaula de voces y ojos encendidos
salvadoreño unos gemían guatemalteco otros
gritaban chiapaneco hombre veracruz tabasco michoacán
así chapaleaban las voces de cada uno
como si tuvieran naciones
como si tuvieran terrenos
como si tuvieran países
tantas voces escurrían por esas ventanas locas
ese humo sin carbón
pero nunca llegó
el señor coyote el señor estaba
bajo las láminas y cilindros estaba
brindando cervezas y rollos de mariachi
estaba en la mesa
con sus cuates sus chidos
volaba sobre el pequeño circo de ese pueblo
en las montañas más arriba que la nada
probando tacos al pastor de pierna sesos
de tripa milanesa de buche y gallina
de lomo de longaniza y chicharrón
carcajeándose con su boca llena de maíz
y su camisa de cowboy aceitada color de rosas
uno por uno dos por dos
se escaparon
uno por uno
dos por dos
eras jorge
eras margarita
eras vicente y florencio
eras alma y esperanza

una esposa un joven solo
con los ojos hinchados
con grietas en los labios
la garganta cerrada las piernas
arañadas sin planeta sin estación
era verano era todo el tiempo de pizca
era verano eterno candente tiempo
sin tiempo de resucitar como gigantes
para regresar al sur un día
así se fueron
uno por uno
dos por dos
eran catorce eran seis
sin agua
sin pan
sin nombre
sin licencia
sin papeles
sin cartera
sin estrellas
un camión de sombras y jinetes
unos arrastrados debajo
otros atrás
otros más abajo
otras en la cajuela
otros con la espalda contra el motor
quemándose la piel
ardiendo y gritando
derritiéndose gota a gota
brazo por brazo

pero nadie los oía
nadie
se daba cuenta
sólo las llantas chillando
sólo los filamentos cromados de los metales
raspando el asfalto hacia el norte
sólo la noche selva
hecha de alambres jirafas rifles joyas
uno por uno
dos por dos
eras maría
y juana y norma y teresa
eras francisco apolonio fernando roberto
se montaron en otro camión
al fin vamos llegando hermano
mira ves la hacemos hermanita
así se hablaban medio dormidos
medios muertos y enterrados
los aprehendieron en una garita
y los soldados hablaron
de dónde eres muchacho
dime de cuál pueblo
preguntaron los verdes
soy mexicano
soy mexicano
soy mexicano
uno por uno dijeron
luego dos
por dos
eran veinticinco

eran catorce
yo sé de dónde vienes
y pa' dónde vas bájate
o si no te bajo yo
y así cayeron
con sus faldas hechas trizas
con sus huaraches y
zapatos de hebras
y los metieron en la cárcel
unos hicieron llamadas
otros
se quedaron tirados sin aliento
a unos los sacaron
los hermanos o una tía
los demás
golpeados se hincaron en la tierra
con sus ojos sin agua
fríos apagados y sus manos
infladas duras de quince años
de veinte de diecinueve de cincuenta y seis así
solos en esos rotos esqueletos quítate
la blusa quítate las pantaletas
vamos a ver qué traes allí
y nadie supo nada
y nadie
dijo nada
tomando café con leche
en las oficinas nadie
los buscó
los otros salieron corriendo

era noche de lotería sin reintegro
era un desierto que no se acababa
y gritaron solos
al fin estoy libre
al fin me voy a los estados
quiero ganar unos centavos
unos cuantos billetitos para
mi madre y mis hijos y
una pick-up chevrolet pero no del año y
corrían hacia las luces
amarillas y rojas y azules y blancas
como fuego y alarmas en ese salitre
hielo y flama a la misma vez
pero esas luces se apagaron
eran más patrullas más soldados
y los enjaularon
en la celda otra vez
uno por uno
dos por dos
eran tantos que parecían
el desierto mismo
destrozado negro color humo
y las olas de voces y sangre corrían
cada noche sólo los sostenía
una rendija del paisaje un abanico de llantos
ese abismo en el que nacieron
sin nombre sin memoria
sólo un calor distante
un eco de la nada que sufrían
unos salieron y apenas podían ver

otros se quedaron bajo las sombras
y allí se ahogaron en el mar de las celdas
uno por uno
dos por dos
eran treinta
eran cinco
eran eternos un esposo
uno quería ser estudiante
quería libros para estudiar
quería lucir un traje azul de contador
una quería una casita
otra quizás aprender inglés
uno por uno
entraron al desierto
parecía méxico
sin piel de jaguares
guatemala sin
lagunas ni volcanes
parecía puerto libertad
pero sin agua ni remo
parecía janitzio pero sin su verde azul
cruzaron uno por uno
dos por dos
miguela de once años
maría dolores garcía lópez quintana carrillo
y más nombres como martínez álvarez garza avina
monreal sifuentes smith corona un esposo
un joven un muchacho
perdido buscando a su madre otro
miró hacia arriba y notó los claveles blancos

son nubes de lluvia son las palabras de dios
es un barco de ilusión así decían cuando
cruzaron por las arenas rojas
por los bejucos
hasta que cayeron
en la ranchería de los papago
a millas de agua prieta naco
y más allá de tucson
hasta que se perdieron
en aquellas casuchas
del gobierno encogidas
por el fuego azul del cielo
unos se quedaron atrás escarbando
raspando la tierra
sabe a lluvia
sabe a leche
y allí cerraron los ojos
las pestañas erizadas
para siempre
otros
se escondieron
en casas laminadas de los indios los robaron
abrieron las camas y las petacas y nada
encontraron en las cajitas de listones
sólo ceniza y más sombras más arenas
nada y todo
uno por uno siguieron
el camino hacia ningún rumbo hacia
un sueño sin tierra sin horizonte
sus labios perdidos sus manos cortadas

sus corazones sólo sus corazones
quedaban pero ya no eran corazones
vacíos de sangre
o ritmo de aliento
era un árbol anciano
que nacía del pecho
un alma
de ramas anaranjadas y nidos morados
rotos sin miel sólo hojas
espinas huesos sombras fuegos
luego se abrió la tierra de secas luces
y más patrullas y más celdas y más hornos
uno por uno
dos por dos
estoy vivo
o estoy soñando
estoy muerto así decían
esos cuerpos
cruzando
desiertos tras desiertos
mira las flores y los ríos
la lluvia fina y fuentes y gallinas y ferias
los jardines el cielo limpio las casas nuestras los
platillos de panes y flanes y salsas y frijoles y
regalitos y el caballo del ranchito
y el pozo lleno y las risas de maría y pedro
y josé y marianito maruch
saludándose uno por uno
dos por dos entraron acariciando
a sus hijos y sus perritos cansados

quemando destrozando el horizonte de veredas
y milpas rotas
cuando vivían en otro tiempo en otra vida
así llegaron a donde empezaron
uno por uno
dos por dos
sus bocas
picadas por abejas
sus manos casi como tocando guitarras
cruzadas sobre el pecho
en cajas sin nombre
entre tablas secas
color vino color de nunca siempre
envueltos en sábanas extranjeras
    sus labios medio abiertos casi bebiendo agua
    sus cabelleras delgadas brillantes saludándose
        en el viento

Obra nueva

Kundalini Spirit Growl

AZTLÁN CHRONICLES, VOL. 3, NO. 7

The sacred lies behind the navel of the body, in front of
the forehead, in between the ulna & the humerus, somewhere
in the arc of ribs & eyelids, in the sex center, in the
lotus-shaped flora of brain & tongue, the nipple, throat &
the chin, there it rises in kundalini spirit growl, the
city-system flourishes with the sweat of this body sacred,
then it cuts it down again & again the body replenishes
itself, replaces itself, reaches mitosis, the others from
itself, becomes the others-from-itself. That is all it knows
this body sacred in blue breath hustling across cloud smog
& red light honks & jackhammers bowing with one syllable
blast between heaven & sky

LIMPIA

Circa 1993-2007

LIMPIA FOR WALKING INTO CLEAR CAMPOS

Winter, Carbondale, Illinois.
Late February 1993.

Step ahead, be careful—the ice,
You can slip.

Loosen up, breathe. Remember to breathe deep.
Unfasten. Swing to an easy beat.
Let your jacket become light, the sweet light
from the floating leaves of winter.
Sing to yourself. Follow the naked trees.
Sing

I drop my burdens
from my feet that guide them
I drop my burdens
from my ankles that turn them
I drop my burdens
from my calves that cup them
I drop my burdens
from my knees that rock them
I drop my burdens
from my tights that run them

I drop my burdens
from my hips that churn them
I drop my burdens
from my sex that heats them
I drop my burdens
from my belly that smoothes them
I drop my burdens
from my ombligo that ties them
I drop my burdens
from the small of my back that cradles them
I drop my burdens
from my cintura that dances them
I drop my burdens
from my ribs that cage them
I drop my burdens
from my breast that nourishes them
I drop my burdens
from my mid-back that protects them
I drop my burdens
from my shoulder blades that build them
I drop my burdens
from my shoulders that salute them
I drop my burdens
from my upper arms that wrap them
I drop my burdens
from my elbows that swing them
I drop my burdens
from my forearms that carry them
I drop my burdens
from my wrists that pull them

I drop my burdens
from my hands that grasp them
I drop my burdens
from my fists that defend them
I drop my burdens
from my fingers that find them
I drop my burdens
from my neck that balances them
I drop my burdens
from my head that circles them
I drop my burdens
from my forehead that honors them
I drop my burdens
from my eyes that picture them
I drop my burdens
from my nose that breathes them
I drop my burdens
from my face that covers them
I drop my burdens
from my lips that invite them
I drop my burdens
from my mouth that savors them
I drop my burdens
from my voice that soothes them
I drop my burdens
from my throat that swallows them
I drop my burdens
from my heart that lives them
I drop my burdens
from my lungs that fill them

I drop my burdens
from my stomach that knots them
I drop my burdens
from my body that holds them
I drop my burdens.
I drop my burdens.
As I walk, I drop my burdens.
As I walk, I melt with the snow.

From *Notebooks of a Chile Verde Smuggler*, 2004.

34 THINGS I DID AFTER MY MOTHER DIED

For Andre.

I stepped out of the San José Hospital at midnight 14ᵗʰ Street to
Original Joe's on Second Street ate pasta tasted nothing I shaved my
head slipped on a ragged mustard gas protection trenchcoat I bought
at Thrift-town on Mission Street strolled SF Bay with Margarita Robles
& Victor Martinez let the wind howl through me I could not hear it I
visited F. D. the therapist who asked me to speak to the empty chair &
announce to my dead father that my mother had died I jogged the
Rose Garden on Taylor Street shouting names & sweating hours I
wanted to keep forever I drove her tiny box of ashes home & felt the
knife I dreamed a rolling wave swelling then she handed me a gift at
the peak of a green hill that unraveled the map of my life to come I
wrote things into a journal like F. D. the therapist said the sufferings I
could not take my eyes off of them I caught more dreams like the dark
house the stove where she brushed next to me lit small days on the
road in trailers & downtown apartments I stared at the nine fotographs
I had of her & made them move I listened to her voice captured
accidentally for half a second on a cassette recorder I let water stream
down my face while I drove the 101 south from San Francisco I
replayed her last breath how it slipped away as if a secret parable yet so
simple I kept coming back to the long-time pain the sufferings my eyes
lost something I talked about her death to students in my class at De
Anza to strangers on the street I called on my aunt Alvina Quintana

who I had not seen for decades & she came to the tiny memorial where
I read a short poem I walked the sidewalks she had walked & saw her at
bus stops going nowhere I opened my arms toward the sky & knelt on
small mounds of earth I noticed I could have a conversation with her in
that other realm I realized my partner's mother Dolores Robles was my
second mother I invited my father Felipe back again & his ancient life
his sombrero & his stories I ambled to the south and searched for my
grandmother Juanita Martinez's grave at Evergreen Cemetery touched
it & bowed down in the El Paso air I read a poem of colors for my aunt
Alvina when it was her time in '02 I noticed the years move across the
walls five ten fifteen twenty after ten something on the left side of my
chest burst into a leaf I began to read the clouds & strewn stones &
torn broken branches I listened to everything speak in her familiar
careful patient fiery voice I read a long poem for my second mother
Dolores Robles when it was her time in '06 I ambled down the avenues
leaving so many things behind I was a man I smoothed my hands on
the table & noticed their shape their softness I read a poem for my
youngest cousin Rosita María Quintana when it was her time at the end
of '06 I realized Rosita was made of small things as my mother how she
spoke to flowers the way my mother spoke to birds I gazed at my
cousin's sixteen-year-old son Andre left to wander & wonder as I was
left at 16 by my father's passing I embraced him I let my pace shift on
its own the way clouds part & merge again into new forms I splashed
cologne on my face & neck like my mother used to & laughed a little

I kept her gifts close to me—then I gave them away

New work

THE SOUL IS A BONE

The spirit is a bone.
Hegel

The soul is a bone
    The soul is a bone
    The soul is a bone
  That is why when it fractures only you can gather the pieces
The soul is a bone
    The soul is a bone
    The soul is a bone
  That is why when the moon-wolf howls you lose your breath
The soul is a bone
    The soul is a bone
    The soul is a bone
  That is why when you knock-knock against your sternum it rises
The soul is a bone
    The soul is a bone
    The soul is a bone
  That is why when it is stolen by a moonwitch you bleed desire eternal
The soul is a bone
    The soul is a bone
    The soul is a bone
  That is why when someone close to you perishes
    the crystal column splinters
    wings for the ascent

New work

On Blood & Power

AZTLÁN CHRONICLES, VOL. 1, NO. 17

The day came when I stripped it down to two things two
things just two things that is what it is this globalist
American experience about this cultural miasma this society
that says it is a society & yet is barely in its first
stages where it doesn't know or see or smell or taste or
hold or conjure peace what is it then what is it then it
occurred to me as if in a chorus all things calling me at
the same time calling out here here they said a super-power
is always engaged in the uncanny reproduction of power-for-
itself & the core-center where this power resides is the
actual blood of things the blood of peoples the blood of
sentient natures

PUNK HALF PANTHER

Circa 1999

PUNK HALF PANTHER

For Oloberto & Magritta, my Geminis.
For Ginsberg.

Lissen
to the whistle of night bats—
oye como va,
in the engines, in the Chevys
& armed Impalas, the Toyota gangsta'
monsters, surf of new world colony definitions
& quasars & culture prostars going blam

   over the Mpire, the once-Mpire, carcass
neural desires for the Nothing. i amble
outside the Goddess mountain. Cut across
the San Joaquín Valley, Santiago de Cuba,
Thailand & Yevtushenko's stations;
hunched humans snap off cotton heads
gone awry & twist
nuclear vine legs.

Jut out to sea, once again—this slip
sidewalk of impossible migrations. Poesy mad
& Chicano-style undone wild.

Rumble boy. Rumble girl.

In wonder & amazement. On the loose.
Cruisin' shark-colored maze of presidential bombast, death
enshrined archipelago fashion malls, neutered wars
across the globe come barreling down
on my Neo-American uzi mutations, my upgraded
2Pac thresholds. My indigo streets, i say

with disgust & erotic spit, Amerikaner frontier consciousness
gone up long ago. Meet my barriohood, meet me
with the froth i pick up everyday & everyday
i wipe away with ablution & apologia & a smirk, then
a smile on my Cholo-Millennium liberation jacket.

No motha', no fatha',
no sista', no brotha'.
Just us in the genetic ticktock
culture chain, this adinfinitum, clueless Americana
grid of inverted serapes, hallucinations of a nation,
streets in racist Terminator
coagulation.

Get loose
after the day-glo artery of a fix.
Power outages propel us into cosmos definition,
another forty-million-New-Dollar-Plantation Basilica,
or is it tender chaos?

My upside-down
Kahlúa gallon *oración* drool
blackish metal flake desires, the ooze of Dulcinea—

Tepeyac stripper, honey
from Tara's open green fans. Tara?

Tara, where are you?
Tara of the blessings & weapons against illusion.
Against administrator pig,
against molester snake,
against rooster corporate lust. Remember me?
i am the black-red blood spark worker,
Juana Buffalo's illegitimate flight usher,
back up from *Inframundo.*

Quick ooze again,
this formless city space
i live in—
my circular false malaria.

Fungi Town says everything's awright
without your Holy Wheel,
your flaming tree wombs, this sista' bundle
i ache for, the one i lost

in a fast brawl for redemption
at the gates of this Creation Mulatto Hotel,
this body passage, this wonder
   fire from the chest.

i stand alone on Mass Man Boulevard.
Look east, look south. Bleary sirens
come howling with vats of genocide &

grey prison gang buses jam
with my true brotha' wetbacks.

Pick another bale of tropical grape,
another bushel of pesticide & plutonium artichoke.
Cancer tomatoes the biggest in the world.
Bastard word, *bracero* produce, alien culture—

      power & slime.
Crawl up my back, heavy
loaded on cheap narratives,
Salinas doubles, Atlantis sketched on Gorbachev's forehead:
you, yes, you, gator-mouthed agent—like gila progeny.
Let's hustle. Let's trade.
It is 1:27 A.M. in da rat Arctic.
What do i trade passion for?

Language escapes me. Passion is smoke.
i dissolve.

It is in my nature to disappear. No sista', no brotha'.
No motha', no soul. This shred iciness is all,
a crazy register that destroys itself into Polaroid,
into a glacial sheet of multicolored border walls.

Let's foam & spin flamey
bluish tears for the Thing-Against-Itself, soul-less soul,
this film word surface. Sing out, baby.
Wobble & bop to town.

Drag yo' hands
across my fine-tuned work train named *Desastre*
en route to Freetown—engineered African shaman houses
smell of licorice, Ebola & famine blood, of hair torn,
of death owls & cancerous alcoholic livers, of babies sucking
this deep night to come,

then—a busted chink of afternoon copper light wakes us,
yo' sista' rolls in with a bag of lemons for Evil Eye,
for the seven-inch ache in her abdomen.
Keep me in stride. You.

i am talking to you, fool. Don't
just sit there stretchin' yo' face.

Tell me why fire yearns for the heart.
Write it down. Say it. Fool. Speak the names.

Conjure the recitations from the coffee cup,
the steel-toe, border-crosser boots.

The grass rips up the morning snow lights, jagged & yellowish.
My AIDS face is hidden. Your rot, my epistemology.

i stand in pure light, a blaze of eyes & arms,
volcanic & solar, autistic, anti-written,
burned by mad friars & clerics, uptown
octopi readers, my long hair falls as reddish honey,
on a naked supple back,
    on breasts small & secretive.

Mystery evades me. Shadows crumble.
Without attention, i locate the love void & yet,
i know all is well. My blood rocks to a bolero
out of rhythm, a firefly's bolero that is,
the one in the dog eye. Hear me
warm up to the multi-night. Scribble poems &
    shout rebuke for the sake of scarred angels,
for Tara, who guides me
in her emeraldine, sequined night of lies.
Hear me now,

kin to the half-collie language that i keep & walk.
Kin now, to the leaves that plunge to the floors;
swivel whiteness without axis, tectonic blasts
without mercy. Straitjackets float on the river infinity.

Pink-skinned fishes stare back
as they evolve into my shape, my babble stream
magnetic juan-foolery. Arm wrestle me
on the soccer lawn, kick me in the balls.
The murder music is for everyone.

    The Last Mayan Acid rock band
    plays Berlin's latest score:

dead trade market systems for the dead proletariats,
rip up from Bangkok to Tenejapa. Everyone is
meaningful & vomits, everyone deposits
a stench pail, into the Cube—

Neo-America,
without the fissure of intimate thighs. Cross over into fire,
hunger & spirit. i write on my hand:
the road cuts into a star. Go, now, go, fool.
In your lyric wetback saxophone, the one yo' mama left you,
the Thing-Against-Itself strapped across your hips.

Do not expect me
to name—this Thing-Against-Itself. Play it. Screw it.
Howl up to the Void, the great emptiness,
the original form.

Night Journal:
Keep on rockin', blues fish, in the gauze of the day into night. Out there
somewhere, Dis-America, pick up a chrome bone, the shards of the last
  Xmas
Presidential extravaganza. You, of course, fool.

Swivel into the clear. Float over the greenish migrant barracks pocked
with wire torsos, toes wiggle & predict our forthcoming delirium—
there is a velvet panther shouting out OM in funk, there is a tawny word
in the middle of the city thoroughfare, a planetary semi of lives slices
the wet animal in half. i am that punk half panther. My fierce skull &
mandible, formidable, my pelt is exact as witch quartz, a slashed leg
tumbles down the highway, battered by every dirty, steel wheel. Face up
to the sky, you, i said, to the brilliant gossip from the Goddess parade.
Outside, outside.

So.

Crawl up, baby, come on, keep on floatin'—
slidin', always: for black journeys, always in holiness.

From *Border-Crosser With a Lamborghini Dream,* 1999.

BLOOD ON
THE WHEEL

*Ezekiel saw the wheel,
way up in the middle of the air.*
Traditional gospel song

Blood on the night soil man en route to the country prison
Blood on the sullen chair, the one that holds you with its pleasure

Blood inside the quartz, the beauty watch, the eye of the guard
Blood on the slope of names & the tattoos hidden

Blood on the Virgin, behind the veils,
Behind-in the moon angel's gold oracle hair

 What blood is this, is it the blood of the worker rat?
 Is it the blood of the clone governor, the city maid?
 Why does it course in s's & z's?

Blood on the couch, made for viewing automobiles & face cream
Blood on the pin, this one going through you without any pain

Blood on the screen, the green torso queen of slavering hearts
Blood on the grandmother's wish, her tawdry stick of Texas

Blood on the daughter's breast who sews roses
Blood on the father, does anyone remember him, bluish?

Blood from a kitchen fresco, in thick amber strokes
Blood from the baby's right ear, from his ochre nose
What blood is this?

Blood on the fender, in the sender's shoe, in his liquor sack
Blood on the street, call it Milagro Boulevard, Mercy Lanes #9
Blood on the alien, in the alligator jacket teen boy Juan

There is blood, there, he says
Blood here too, down here, she says
Only blood, the Blood Mother sings

Blood driving miniature American queens stamped into rage
Blood driving rappers in Mercedes blackened & whitened in news
Blood driving the snare-eyed professor searching for her panties
Blood driving the championship husband bent in Extreme Unction

Blood of the orphan weasel in heat, the Calvinist farmer in wheat
Blood of the lettuce rebellion on the rise, the cannery worker's
prize

Blood of the painted donkey forced into prostitute zebra,
Blood of the Tijuana tourist finally awake & forced into pimp sleep
again

It is blood time, Sir Terminator says,
It is blood time, Sir Simpson winks,
It is blood time, Sir McVeigh weighs.

Her nuclear blood watch soaked, will it dry?
His whitish blood ring smoked, will it foam?
My groin blood leather roped, will it marry?
My wife's peasant blood spoked, will it ride again?

Blood in the tin, in the coffee bean, in the *maquila oración*
Blood in the language, in the wise text of the market sausage
Blood in the border web, the penal colony shed, in the bilingual yard

Crow blood blues perched on nothingness again
fly over my field, yellow-green & opal
Dog blood crawl & swish through my sheets

Who will eat this speckled corn?
Who shall be born on this Wednesday war bed?

Blood in the acid theatre, again, in the box office smash hit
Blood in the Corvette tank, in the crack talk crank below

Blood boat Navy blood glove Army ventricle Marines
in the cookie sex jar, camouflaged rape whalers
Roam & rumble, investigate my Mexican hoodlum blood

Tiny blood behind my Cuban ear, wine colored & hushed
Tiny blood in the death row tool, in the middle-aged corset
Tiny blood sampler, tiny blood, you hush up again, so tiny

Blood in the Groove Shopping Center,
In blue Appalachia river, in Detroit harness spleen

Blood in the Groove Virus machine,
In low ocean tide, in Iowa soy bean

Blood in the Groove Lynch mob orchestra,
South of Herzegovina, south, I said

Blood marching for the Immigration Patrol, prized & arrogant
Blood spawning in the dawn break of African Blood Tribes,
    grimacing
& multiple—multiple, I said

Blood on the Macho Hat, the one used for proper genuflections
Blood on the faithful knee, the one readied for erotic negation
Blood on the willing nerve terminal, the one open for suicide

Blood at the age of seventeen
Blood at the age of one, dumped in a Greyhound bus

Blood mute & autistic & cauterized & smuggled Mayan
& burned in border smelter tar

          Could this be yours? Could this item belong to you?
          Could this ticket be what you ordered, could it?

    Blood on the wheel, blood on the reel
    Bronze dead gold & diamond deep. Blood be fast.

From *Border-Crosser With a Lamborghini Dream*, 1999.

ABANDONED BLOOD

Gone to the drooler dungeon, the mother's buried kitchen, that is.
Gone to the steeple, precise, greenish, the father's abuse, that is.
Gone to the dog pelt infestation, the evening ruffled with sex, that is.
Gone to the taxi gypsy dressed in magic, the last glimpse of his thigh,
    that is.
Gone to the corporate xylophone jazz, the governor's pimp
    plantation, that is.
Gone to the pimple ruby girl clerkship, the fast daughter's suicide,
    that is.
Gone to the Greenback Queen of "C" Street, your aunt, the illegal,
    that is.
Gone to the half-moon, busted eye, the trunk orphan, smuggled,
    that is.
Gone to the lesson of Jew massacres, the sickle through your hair,
    that is.
Gone to the short viola, enchanted, the boy rape stuffed into the ear,
    that is.
Gone to the great emptiness, inside the ring, your last death, of
    course, that is.

From *Border-Crosser With a Lamborghini Dream*, 1999.

BLOOD GANG CALL

Calling all tomato pickers,
   the ones wearing death frowns instead of jackets
Calling all orange & lemon carriers,
   come down the ladder to this hole
Calling all chile pepper sack humpers,
   you, yes, you the ones with a crucifix
Calling all garlic twisters
   caught in the winter spell of frozen sputum
Calling all apple tossers
   high up in the heaven of pesticides, stick faced
Calling all onion priests
   & onion nuns & onion saints killing for rain
Calling all tobacco pullers,
   thick leaf rollers in the ice burn of North Carolina
Calling all melon pitchers
   in the rivet machine, in the assembly bed of bones
Calling all artichoke pressers
   kneeling at the mount of signs chanting OM
Calling all peach slicers
   preserving shells in the form of a tiny orange fetus
Calling all lettuce skirts
   kicking lust down to the underworld soul prison
Calling all watermelon shiners
   paring the sugary womb in search of Goddess

Calling all cotton pilots
    seeding the froth on my mother's grave, rebellious
Calling all strawberry weavers
    threading your wire mesh heart with thorns
Calling all tomato pickers,
    the old ones, wearing frayed radiator masks.

From *Border-Crosser With a Lamborghini Dream*, 1999.

NYC, 1999

AZTLAN CHRONICLES, VOL. 5, NO. 5

Picked up the paper in Manhattan then I opened the enve-
lope where one of my agents told me Hey Juan I like this
manuscript but I gotta tell you this one the latest one
well it's like you are just writing notes to yourself then
I leaned back opened this photo see my Uncle Chente in the
'30s he is sitting on an apple crate somewhere on a New
York City sidewalk with a sombrero a mustache laughing in
front of his sunsanded gallery of paintings & caricatures
for exhibit for sale for anyone passing through Vicente
Quintana the man from barrio Niño Perdido Mexico City
early 1900s white shirt black pants smiling under the
rough hat across time

104 THINGS A CHICAN@ STREET POET WORRIES ABOUT

Circa 1999

DON'T WORRY, BABY

*This one's for you, Carrillo & Sifuentes &
García & Silberg & Clavillazo.*

I worry about comedians who call me to back up their old
    Communisms
I worry about teen Chicanas advertising Jehovah at the bakery
I worry about exotic birds learning too much English
I worry about Subcomandante Marcos getting acne under the ski
    mask
I worry about feminists who want to identify Cubans in the room
I worry about tourists who think maids are natural
I worry about the governor's face muscles
I worry about disc jockeys who feel "enemy music" is a game
I worry about the Dalai Lama strolling into a Sicilian seafood
    restaurant
I worry about writing workshops using hacksaws
I worry about Bill Cosby's karma
I worry about the return of folk singers
I worry about people who use the word *folk*
I worry about OJ's parenting methods
I worry about E. coli in Congress
I worry about Spielberg's next ethnic movie
I worry about New Age music repeating itself
I worry about drive-bys low on gas
I worry about the high cholesterol of mariachis

I worry about soybeans invading Chicago
I worry about congueros who use Vaseline
I worry about little boys who memorize surgical procedures
I worry about Black and White panels
I worry about the flakes in the breakfast cereals
I worry about what an elevator does to men
I worry about the receding hairline of trees
I worry about the innate anger of clouds
I worry about Zen priests dolled up in Hugo Boss suits
I worry about jazz running out of improvisations
I worry about Beijing doing Elvis
I worry about Russian women becoming rednecks
I worry about ethnics who claim four races
I worry about computers with bomb icons
I worry about artists who emphasize the word *visual*
I worry about Mexicans digging their stereotypes
I worry about X-mas sales in May
I worry about poets who believe in publishing
I worry about the word *alien* becoming too familiar
I worry about churches looking sharper than Macy's
I worry about the ass on the other side of the glass ceiling
I worry about the day having hours, minutes and seconds
I worry about children with careers
I worry about conversations turning into exhibits
I worry about the continuous supply of tomatoes
I worry about fast food in prison
I worry about impatient stop signs
I worry about brain shaving
I worry about battery-operated suicide machines
I worry about couples who date

I worry about greenhouse gases escaping from the White House

I worry about Stephen King's supply of vitamin D

I worry about cigars rolled in Maine

I worry about trendy transfusions

I worry about Oprah's penchant for T-shirt bedsheets

I worry about performance art going into the poultry business

I worry about kindergarten teachers whose clothes match

I worry about copy-cat do-gooders

I worry about the DNA chain getting loose

I worry about husbands on the phone

I worry about glossy 8x10 murder snapshots

I worry about nurses with no pay hikes

I worry about the dishwasher's revenge

I worry about assembly plants making plans

I worry about a faster way to process fries

I worry about tacos, pizza, ribs, and bagels running out of steam

I worry about old fogies who stand up for the King of Beers

I worry about insurance agents posing as poets

I worry about a soprano sax replacing the mood of pain

I worry about smog in my retina

I worry about the complexion of beans

I worry about forces that get armed

I worry about the Mexican baker's death wish

I worry about oyster bars going straight

I worry about pro-life men with bulging Bibles

I worry about blues without color

I worry about sex without sardines and cream soda

I worry about cut flowers on dirty graves

I worry about nuns with extra-large shoes

I worry about the seriousness of high-grade mascara

I worry about the Gauguin poster in the coroner's office
I worry about recruiters searching for color
I worry about carbohydrate lobotomies
I worry about rock cocaine as a vocational mining industry
I worry about smiling obituaries
I worry about the interpretation of death-row graffiti
I worry about the liverwurst in Bangkok
I worry about monolingual emergency signs
I worry about friendly status countries
I worry about the word *poet* being replaced by the word *Narodnik*
I worry about VFW halls that have Taco Thursdays
I worry about dancing in front of meat-eating seagulls
I worry about walnuts that resemble human innards
I worry about guys locked up so they can write
I worry about Picasso Tupperware
I worry about the army's knowledge of mountains
I worry about cowboys in rocket ships
I worry about rappers entering a spelling bee
I worry about the dead never speaking up
I worry about chickens in robot suits
I worry about the third kiss
I worry about proms as delivery rooms
I worry about high school cafeterias as artillery ranges
I worry about what I am saying
I worry about the word *Mexican* having an X
I worry about people who say "Don't worry, baby."

From *Notebooks of a Chile Verde Smuggler*, 2004.

American Things

AZTLÁN CHRONICLES, VOL. 4, NO. 2

There I am at the Feil Building second floor flat rockin'
1983 Folsom & Van Ness Mission District San Francisco
again my charred powder yellow van with its generator
burnt parked outside I am on the tile with my head rubbing
against an EZ chair a microphone by my belly honking poems
with congas by John Martinez Fresno marauder & Jack
Hirschman splishes Russian verses by Mayakovsky enumera-
tions of things to come the street the time the news too
much news on the planet the night the heat the rap the beat
the skin the sound the grains in the wood the legs & feet
sugary & akimbo the regimes the smoke the mist Potrero
Hill the winds rush in the molecules Santana has touched
my little mother in my apartment the murals of '82 on 24th
Street dripping the love the flesh the breath the sales
machines the adding machines the shoes next to my face
drowning out the dawn the military en route the true gar-
den behind every Victorian downstairs the grasses meowing
this very minute as you wail or was it 1981 I am jabbin' a
busted sonnet in iambic in eighteen-syllable lines gotta
do something original for the reading at the Grand Piano
on Haight Street that geranium-scented ribbon of '67 gotta
write it as fast as I can gotta be able to sing it back-
wards forwards with a beat with a locking beat in my blue
tweed speckled dinner coat gyroscope the audience throw-
ing a torqued shuffle across América

ARE YOU DOING THE NEW AMERIKAN THING?

Circa 1978-1982

LETANÍA PARA JOSÉ ANTONIO BURCIAGA

October 13, 1996.
At the old Victoria Theater in S.F.
on 16th Street where I used to
see Clavillazo & Luis Aguilar movies
while eating lobby chicharrones
in the early sixties.
This one's for you, Tony.

Ese Burciaga,
      Vato de la divina tórica, vato escuadra
Ruega por nosotros
Ese vato muralista, con delantal de panadero
      Hacedor de pinturas y nuestras historias en paredones
ilegales
Ruega por nosotros
Ese Tin-Tan del Chuko
Ruega por nosotros
      Buzo del segundo barrio, casa zapata y de menlo parque
Ruega por nosotros
Ese poeta de la plebe bilingüe
      Escritor de milpa, misterio y esmelda
Ruega por nosotros
Ese tarjetero, cuate de vecindades
      En firme comunicación, cercos sueltos y campesinos al aire
Ruega por nosotros
Ese vato, compañero de la Cecilia

Jefito del Toño y la Rebecca, hermano de la onda bronca
Ruega por nosotros
Ese cholo de monterey
Con lapices y acrílicos y mantequilla y esperanza en la brocha
Ruega por nosotros
Ese burciaga
Tirador de botellas de colores contra los fiscales y sus changos
Ruega por nosotros
Ese cantinchuko
De bolsa Tijuanera, sacos de chiles chicanos y chistes de lobo
Ruega por nosotros
Ese tony
Profe del tomate, de la sierra en protesta y de los jarochos
Ruega por nosotros
Ese vato apasionado
Con letras locas, los nombres de los olvidados y
Movimientos por la justicia
Ruega por nosotros
Ese compa de los compas
Con los burritos mochos y las tortillas frisbees pa'lonche
Ruega por nosotros
Ese silkscreen beret
Tomando cultura y corazón en vez de Coca-Cola
Ruega por nosotros
Ese carnal con el fonazo político
Con la voz urgente y las tardeadas en tu cantón al lado del
101
Ruega por nosotros
Ese homey del sol total
Trozo de pan familiar y luz naciente sobre la mesa del barrio

Ruega por nosotros
Ese jornalero de tinta
  Voz para el pueblo, vos de oro y conciencia, voz del pobre
Ruega por nosotros
Ese cura con la corbata al revés
  Sembrando letanías y amores, milagros sociales y flores
Ruega por nosotros
Ese poetazo de adobe
  De pinole y pozole y curaciones y marchas a medianoche
Ruega por nosotros
Ese vatín alivianando
  De camiseta tipo camaleón, ascendiente de Juariles
Ruega por nosotros
Ese vato machín con la guayavera tucked-in
  Jalando con estudiantes y hermanas carmelitas hasta el
amanecer
Ruega por nosotros
Ese burgie
  Armando tertulias, rondallas, barbequiadas y lunadas de
hermandad
Ruega por nosotros
Ese tony con Tony Lamas del Río Grande
  En El Bracero bar, en Madera Roja, dibujando las verdades
Ruega por nosotros
Ese jacalero de mi cora, cantando
  San Antonio en vez de "santone"
El Paso del Norte en vez de Elpasowe
Sabes que, carnal José Antonio, la verdad es que me canso
  Me canso de no verte
  Me canso de no escucharte

De no sentir tu ternura a mi lado
Pero yo te recuerdo
Y no me olvido, la verdad es que
No sé más que no olvidarte
No sé más que siempre escucharte
En esta vereda aquí

Ese Burciaga, ese padrino del divino bolo, ese alacrán buti suave
Aquí te cantamos, en caló, en calor y puro amor.

Amen, Awimmin
Y con safos.

From *Notebooks of a Chile Verde Smuggler*, 2004.

ARE YOU DOING THE NEW AMERIKAN THING?

For all movement, ex-movement and anti-movement affiliates and
for Brandi Treviño, 1978,

Are you doing that new Amerikan thing?
Sweet thing, handsome thing, that thing about coming out, all the
    way out
About telling her, her telling him, telling us, telling them that we
Must kill the revolutionary soul, because it was only a magical thing
A momentary thing, a thing outside of time, a sixties thing, a sacred
    thing
A brown beret thing, a grassroot thing, a loud thing, a spontaneous
    thing
A Viet Nam thing, a white radical thing, an Aztlán thing, a Cholo thing
A nationalist thing, a for Pochos only thing, a college thing, an
    August 29, 1970
Chicano Moratorium thing, an outdated thing, a primitive thing.

Sweet thing, handsome thing, that thing about coming out, all the
    way out
On a Communist scare thing, a Red thing, a let's go back to war thing
Because we must stop the El Salvador thing because it could lead to
    another
      Nicaragua

Thing because we need Reagan and Order in the Américas thing.

Are you doing that new Amerikan thing?

The chains, pins and leather thing
The aluminum thing
The transparent plastik underwear thing
The lonely boulevard thing
The hopeless existentialist thing
The neo-Paris melancholy thing
The nightmare thing
The urban artist thing
The laughing thing
The serious suicide thing
The New Amerikan Chicano thing
The end of the world thing
The victim thing
The enlightened quasi-political thing
The university hustle for the pie thing
The *We Are the Community* thing

Are you doing that new Amerikan thing?

The *nacimos para morir* thing
The *yo te protejo* thing
The *Dios y Hombre* thing
The *quién sabe* thing
The *así nomás* thing
The *todo se acaba* thing
The *la vida es un misterio* thing

The *quisiera ser* thing
The *vato firme* thing
The *chavala de aquellas* thing
The *no me toques* thing
The *no quiero problemas* thing

Are you doing that new Amerikan thing?

Doing the be clean be seen by the right people thing
Doing the be macho again because women like it anyway thing
Doing the look out for number one because you tried the group
    thing thing
Doing the be submissive again because after all a woman needs a man
    thing
Doing the Army thing because it really pays more than hanging
    around the Barrio thing
Doing the women's draft thing because you can do it better than the
    men thing
Doing the purity thing because no one got to be president by eating
    greasy tacos
    thing
Doing the spa thing because there you will meet the right tall & dark
    & blond & tender thing
Doing the homophobic thing because you caught yourself lusting at
    an abberration thing

Are you doing that new Amerikan thing?

Sweet thing, handsome thing, that thing about coming out, all the
    way out

About telling her, her telling him, telling us, telling them that we
Must kill the revolutionary soul?

From *Exiles of Desire*, 1983.

In Hach Winik Sugar, 1993

AZTLÁN CHRONICLES, VOL. 6, NO. 21

In '69 the goddess of fire egged me on I was in Nichol-
son's anthro class at UCLA an EOP boy peach-fuzz-faced in
the back row yellow legal paper pad & red ink pen thinking
about nothing or the next party at the crazy aha-Chicano
pad we had slipped into after we shut the university down
on strike with MECHA & the Black Student Union & SDS with
Zeta Acosta handing out his poems in wrinkled 20lb bond &
Ricardo Sanchez was still working on his first book *Canto
y Grito mi Liberación* somewhere in El Paso we reconned in
Santa Monica all nighters in smoke & wine & you know so in
class Professor Nicholson said There are only 250 Lacandón
Mayas—the Hach Winik, True Persons—in Chiapas only 250
left when he said that something came over me I knew there
& then what I had to do one way or the other I knew where
I was headed to over & over a flashy neon liberation film
strip repeated itself the one that pictured hach winik
until I could see it wherever I was seeing it then it hap-
pened again in '93 while I was on a dream quest in
Carbondale, Illinois one mile from the Shawnee forest
where I lived in a beige duplex something's going on some
thing's going on the spirit wind from the ancestral mounds
in that dark hole spoke

ONE YEAR BEFORE THE ZAPATISTA REBELLION

1993

Behind the house K'ayum Ma'ax built. Nahá, Lacandón Jungle.
Chiapas, Mexico, 1993.

ONE YEAR BEFORE THE ZAPATISTA REBELLION

I am going to where I am from.
I am fleeing from visions, fences
grinning from the post. Give me
a hole with a past to it. Fill up
this mess with your wicked engines.

Lorna Dee Cervantes
From "On Touring Her Hometown"

"How can I write about Mexico?" Juan said. He had just returned to California from an arduous trek to Chiapas. "With my bare hands, my two fists—with the guts of the people and gravel bits from the crazy roads." The task punished him and left him without what he seemed to need most—words. Big words embossed with agile meanings that would travel far and land softly on the shoulders of a student, a little girl, maybe a young woman about to reconsider her life or a sturdy professional in the sundry course of office chatter. The silvery words would fall casually into their ears, and then, after a pause, these careful terms would unwrap and explode. Juan wanted this explosion, and yet he had no idea how to light the fuse of letters.

"What about the Indian? Can the writer truly speak of revolution?" Juan smiled a wry smile. He knew that he was about to collapse; there was little room for North American writers to speak of Mexico and its concatenation of Indian archipelagos in a neocolonial choke chain.

Juan's very status as a writer prospering in the ganglia of a superpower sabo-taged his literary claims.

It was starting all over, he could taste it; this uncanny inclination to say something true; to cast out his soul and let it fly in all its multicolored vapors—with language. "Mirrors and mirror games." He laughed and fidgeted.

Juan was well aware that when he talked of Mexico, he was actually talking about Latin America. Juan laughed again. "I must really be stupid," he said. As soon as he mentioned Latin America, he would slip; he knew this. The rhetoric would falter and soon enough he would end up referring to Malaysia or the Philippines; each landscape was interchangeable, Third World borders seemed to be illusory—the border work was more like an Escher pattern superimposed throughout various zones of exploitation throughout the globe.

Juan had just arrived from his journey: Mexico City, Tuxtla Gutiérrez, San Cristóbal de las Casas—the highlands, the lowlands. His lips were parched. Reddish flecks dotted his forehead where the tropical sun of southeastern Chiapas had burned his skin. Was the language on his face?

He was at his desk inside an ordinary three-bedroom suburban house in a small California town. "I have all the clues in my hand, I've had them for God knows how long." It was only last night, after his plane landed in San Francisco, that the pieces of the puzzle finally fell into place. He finally saw how he would gather all his experiences and recast every tiny moment in Chiapas that had whirled through his blood: from San Francisco to San Cristóbal de las Casas, then to

Ocosingo, the gateway into the lowlands, and finally to the Lacandón jungle, to Nahá, one of two major Lacandón Maya villages. Juan meditated on the last vestiges of the lowlands, the wiry and blackened forests; he could see the tawdry rope of slavery and sickness tied around the wrists of every Tzotzil-Tzeltal and Lacandón Maya Indian in the landscape. The double knot of Ladino usury and Indian dependence stood in bold relief. He brushed his dark hair back, propped his glasses over the bridge of his nose. What of the wealthy Ladinos sympathetic to the plight of displaced campesinos and oppressed Indians? And the new class of wealthy Indians who feared any change in the social order that would interfere with their hard-won status? The meditation dissolved.

What writing? What language? Even the term "native" irritated him. He had nothing to say. Pure and simple. Nothing. Juan would have to invent a conversation in order to solve his predicament. An old conversation?

During the early summer of 1970, while living in Santa Monica and attending UCLA, Juan had begun the task of finding the terms for Mexico. These were the acid days, the Chicano movimiento days— Molotov cocktails hurled at Greek frats, high school blowouts in East L.A. and antiwar rallies. These were the days of truth, Quaaludes, and jazzy verbs for liberation. Black Power and salsa-blues bands. Just like that and pow! Juan tasted the flavors of the early seventies: poetry in prisons with a Gibson guitar strapped across his back, riffing with saxophone and congas in farmworker camps. "Pow! Just like that." This was the manner in which Juan headed south from Los Angeles, to the center of the world Mexico, for the first time. Everything pasted onto his eyes: old volumes of anthropology and archaeology on the aesthetics of Bonampak, Frans Blom and Gertrude Duby's 1940s list of jungle expedition supplies, Viet Nam black and green canvas boots, bulk rolls of Ilford film, the degree charts of rain, and the hollow-eyed gaze of the last five hundred Lacandón Mayas.

Now he found it difficult to plow through that romantic jumble. He needed the second conversation, a deeper connection—the circle of native faces, men huddled around little fires at the heights of the Sierra Madre, women praying hard in slanted twig shelters, speaking to the goddess of corn; an odd-shaped Lacandón tortilla from Nahá brushed with chili paste and washed down with a gourd of lemonade. Juan needed these fragile images in order to find his proper stance.

In 1970 in Tepic, Nayarit, Juan had met Ramón Medina Silva, a Huichol shaman who had been waiting for him downtown at the Instituto Nacional Indigenista. "Tauyepá, Father Sun told me that you were coming," Ramón informed him in the outskirts of the mestizo city. "Come back and visit me after you return from Veracruz and Chiapas. When you come back we will look over these yarn paintings and we will talk of the fire, the earth, and the road to the stars, the crystal shapes of the soul. When you come back." Juan left for the Atlantic coast, to northern Veracruz. "Let's say we have a date with someone we forgot on the road long ago," he said to his buddy Tomás when they arrived in Túxpam, in time for the Flying Pole Ceremony of the Totonacs. They stayed and learned about the pole and the ritual fasts of the Totonac youth who lived in Poza Rica, a metropolitan maze of refineries and Ladino merchants, restaurants, and Indian barrios. It was the end of July. The road was half ocean and half ancient shrines, the sea falling away to the left and the jagged trail to Chiapas rising on the right. "No one will believe us when we get back to the States," Juan said to his partner, Tomás. He did not know what awaited them in San Cristóbal de las Casas, in the deeper terrain of la selva. After a month in Chiapas, Juan had set foot in reality. He could not recognize the taste in his mouth—ecstasy, or was it anxiety? Squalor? A buzzing chain of humped humans appeared, some better off than others, rough copper skin shot into black string sandals; men and women like handsome ants with high cheekbones and sleepless eyes, cut with the sharp point of foreign whips and silent centuries—rebellion or oblivion?

After a series of accidents and small triumphs in Mayan country, Juan returned to Ramón in the sierra. Then he lay in the back of a Volkswagen bus, yellowish, bony and fevered; then back in Los Angeles, home, for a while. This was his initiation into the complex of his identities as Chicano, Latino, mestizo, Indian, American—most of all American. Powerlessness in human form: dark-skinned powerlessness at the frayed edges of America; no doubt about it, he had found his Other home too.

For years Juan wandered. "I spent the whole day daydreaming," he would say to his lover. "I found a flower and crushed it against my mouth." "You always do that," Maga, the somber woman with long dark hair, told him. "I wanted to dissolve its colors, to taste true red and true gold. Its little life in my little life." This is how he carried himself. His college friends liked him and confided in him; the rest thought he was a clown, a smart clown good at words. For the next two decades he went about putting up his photos of the distant villages where he had stayed: Nahá, Lacanjá Chan Sayab, Joigelito, Chamula. He spoke of José Pepe Chan Bol, the Mayan Baptist preacher of Lacanjá Chan Sayab, the southern Lacandón village, with his tattered tunic and fine wristwatch, and how they talked about the invasion of chicleros and the rape of their women by Ladinos, and how all the while they were talking they heard the Beatles on a box radio in the night.

"Ramón was different," Juan said. "He was killed in 1971 in the Nayar mountains near his village, El Colorín, a year after I met him. The authorities in Tepic were jealous of him because he was gaining an international audience. Anthropologists and students were flocking to his side. 'These are the secrets,' he would say as he told us the stories of th First Ones. A year later, five shots—dead."

Juan wrote in a frenzy. Poems and antipoems—antipoems most of all. He was fixed on tearing the new language out of the old structures. Juan crossed the streets writing; he stood and wrote holding a miniature paper pad in his hand; jazz and poetry, blues and politics. He wrote on napkins, posters, anything that would take the ink. "I must feed the conversation, the way the Huichol feed Grandfather Fire, Tatewarí, at night, the way the women dance under a full moon, their bare feet on the earth, opal light in their eyes," he told Maga again and again.

In the winter of 1993, Juan journeyed back to Chiapas. "I just have to go," he said to Maga. "I don't know why or what I am going to do when I get there." He had not the slightest inkling that he was about to step into the last days of Chiapas as he had known it. Juan smiled and ambled to the south again, carrying a few bags and a 35 mm camera. He did not know, as he worked himself into the Chiapas lowlands, that a few feet behind his conspicuous figure (as much as he attempted to humble himself in order to slip further into the yellow-green scrim of Indian country) a campesino and Indian revolution hiccupped in the shadows of his fancy-colored backpack.

After a short stay in Chiapas, Juan returned to the States. Again he was caught up with the questions: Where is America? What is an Indian? Who am I? It was an odd maneuver to be a Chicano, a person of color, en route to a "native" topography. The most formidable folly had to do with swallowing the master's conquest language in order to liberate oneself, to initiate the process of resolving one's cultural disenfranchisement in the United States. "I have to become a trickster, a language saboteur," he said. Maybe this was another mirror game. Did he have to become a cross-eyed seeker of self? The path required fracture. He knew, as he had long ago, that first he must disrupt the terms, figures, and images of colonialism if he dared search for the way into America, a path leading back home.

Juan rested his head on Maga's chest and listened to the beating of her heart. "The second conversation," he said softly. Juan realized that he had been lost in the first conversation—the one about loss, genocide, the multiple fissures of America and its native people; the conversation about split cultures and hybrid men and women kicked-in against their Indian selves. Where was their love? The other conversation had not occurred to him. "Machines make love too." Juan could not believe he said this to Maga. Love between machines, between corporate fax voice boxes and military bulldozer teeth. The digitized machine erotica of computer chips and resource exploitation profit lexicons. This was not a language of redemption and social transformation. The terms and channels were corporate and political, and yet it was a language of fire. It ran

181

its yellow-red spikes beyond the borders that riveted America a thousand times over.

The term Indian was not necessary in the second language. "It's funny, Maga. I don't have a word for Indian either, and I am not a machine. How can that be?" No terms for native, America, not even for Mexico—they were all collapsible, they were all quicksilver placeholders for globalized corporate interests. "Useless," he uttered to Maga as he stood up and faced the windows to the southern skies.

"They are like stars," Juan said. Maga knew he was talking about the usurped ones, the sucked-out Indian children, the aged mothers, and the young men with wiry-tree torsos. She stared at him. "Falling stars, rising stars. By the time we see them in their true light, they have shifted into another sky, drifted far out of our reach. Into an unimaginable cosmos of abandonment and power."

"You haven't changed," she said, looking out the window pane with him. "You said you were different now that you are back. But you are still the same man that not too long ago wanted to save a sparrow. Remember, you found it in our backyard? You put it in one of my shoeboxes with a bubble of bread and a small dish of water. You didn't see the claw marks under the wings? Instead, you went to bed and made wild love to me. In the morning, the tiny bird lay on its side, eyes shut, the wings quiet and still. This is your Mexico?"

Juan loosened his shirt collar, peered to the south. He took Maga's hand in his. "They are looking this way too," he said. "From the edges of every border, they look back—mud and cardboard kingdoms, from a busted makeshift hotel they pace; huddled, caught by surprise, by their own hunger and history; a broken hotel, made of smoke, revolution, and the strange intersections of global invasions. In every room there is an Indian, one with a VCR, another with an ancient machete, a missile, a fighting woman, a Ladino on his knees—you and me. Outside, the future lurks and stalks."

Maga nodded her head. "You are quoting yourself, Juan. It is an old poem you wrote years ago. 'The Mexicanos were being lured into a gold hotel,' you said. That's not enough, Juan."

"I suppose you want me to talk about Frida Kahlo?" he asked Maga. "'We are all condemned to be Fridas.' Is that what you want me to say?" He knew Maga's point of view; they had gone over all this with coffee and toast, in blues bars. Juan knew that the central column of our cultural vertebrae had been shattered—much in the same way as Frida's own spine and pelvis had been dismantled in a horrible bus accident when she was eighteen—that we have no unified and authentic discourse of what we are. All we know is that we have been tightened into a cast, our realigned foreign body. And yet, from the inside, we know that we inhabit a radically different space. Juan knew this about Latin America. He also knew that this could be said of any peoples at the margin of power. "Because of the cast and the terrible accidents to our historical selves, we go about immersed in the enterprise of self-portraiture; at every juncture, we seek our shape, our face—right, Maga? Paradox and parody overwhelm us: what we paint is seen as minute and gracious in comparison to the full-bodied enterprise of the master painter, who seems to walk about freely, scale walls, and launch his mediums and letters with such public gaiety and historical intelligibility."

Maga stared: "I know that rap." Juan shrugged his shoulders, sighed. "We are up against everything," Maga said in a deep voice. "Words, concepts, the sly throat of the new Mexican president, our own bogus leadership, if I can use the term leadership at all—the last quarter-inch of topsoil on this continent, the World Bank, Mexican billionaires with NAFTA teacups, military machines in every village; the whole universe when it listens passively; we are up against that too," she said. "Every time we say 'Indian culture' we lose ground, Juan. Every time we say those words we encourage a white-bearded God to wake up, rise and prowl the pyramids and the basalt shrines in search of tropical converts. We give permission to New Age technofriars and culture clerics in diplomatic body wraps to scurry late at night poring over what they have gathered from their devoted Indian informants and most of all from our language about ourselves. How can we speak of a fettered Indian Latin America barely breathing within the inherited boundaries and systems of servitude, finca and hacienda labor credit-debt relations and credit by female rape? Who talks about this? The PRI? Have you heard their shit lately? They are saying that Mexico must honor its cultural patrimony—'honor,' they say, as they divert U.S. antidrug money and World Bank environmental funds for sniper work in the villages. Is this the 'Indian culture' you are talking about? Sparrows? Indians? You would like to put them in the same poem, wouldn't you? How do you talk about your own taste for an Indian paradise? Isn't this what we must fight against too? Have you heard of 'imperialist nostalgia'? It is the modern scurvy of those who live at the margins of this country. You think you are a suburban Zapatista, don't you? Let's see your ammo." They both laughed out loud. Then they both played with their hands and grew silent.

Maruch. San Cristóbal de las Casas, Chiapas. 1970. TOMÁS MENDOZA-HARRELL

Days passed. Juan began to write; Maga worked on a new set of performance art pieces. Maybe the first conversation was his utopian quest in 1970 to the tropical jungle villages of Nahá and Lacanjá Chan Sayab, the story of the last Lacandón in the smoldering forest of charred caoba. Maybe his most recent journey was his second. The third one was locked up in the occasion of a smoldering Mayan and campesino revolution, a Mexico broken and splintered by complex socioeconomic disparities and global interventions. Would he speak of the million Tzotzil, Tzeltal, Tojolabal, and Chol—all the Maya who in many ways were at the mercy of this Lacandón "elite of five hundred" empowered by government environmental concessions and the monetary promise of logging?

"Where is the third conversation, what is it?" Juan asked Maga outside on a city avenue." She gazed hard into his wide-set eyes. "There must be a way to speak, to act," he said. Maga stopped and turned to him. Juan pressed his lips against hers, and for the moment all the words that he had searched for welled up in his heart.

◎　◎　◎

Bor, one of the young sons of Viejo Chan K'in, about sixteen years old and wearing black rubber boots and a tunic, stopped by for a moment in the middle of La Ruta, the front yard of the Lacandones. He was deaf and communicated with a self-invented repertoire of hand signs.

Raised his right hand. Thumb and forefingers fashioned an invisible box. He slapped this sign on his tunic sleeve. An insignia of some sort, on someone's shirt, I thought. Then he spread his left arm, smoothing an upward arc through the air. His hands grasped a steering wheel made out of air. Was he driving? We both laughed as I watched his language.

I liked Bor—his piercing eyes and lithe frame, his finely tapered fingers and his quick smile, his aloneness. He followed the other young boys and played with them. K'ayum Mario, his nephew, spoke to him with a few signs and invited him on several of our jaunts. Bor carried something that the others lacked; maybe it was his inner intensities, maybe it was an extra dose of intimacy with his father and mother, with their day and night worlds. He had cut out the landscape of Nahá in a different manner. I could sense Bor's unique position and way of seeing.

What was the story that he kept repeating—the one about the square box, the imprint on the shirt, and the upward swerve in the sky?

The story came to me: A sergeant's stripes on the sleeve; he came in a plane one day. He drove. They came. Military men with wings and machines. They drove with their badges on their bodies. They went into the villages, into the chozas. They swung their shoulders, their air was metal-like, they came down from the sky. Another sky. The striped badge on their shirts was heavy; it was red and stood out. Everyone in the village saw them, they saw the stripes, the metal on their strong arms. They noticed how they came driving in one day, how they stood tall. How they came and left. Or was this being told to me in a future tense?

Would there be men with stripes on their attire, with machines in the air, with strange jackets on their bodies? How will they hover over Nahá? What will their mission be? Who will live, who will die?

I invented the story as Bor repeated the movements over and over, as he moved his hands over his body and through the space around him. This reminded me of Spielberg's early film, *Close Encounters of the Third Kind*, and how the lead character played by Richard Dreyfuss kept on sculpting towers with his hands, out of mud, and no one understood him; clay towers and mashed-potato towers, until the day came when the tower appeared before him and the rest of the world.

One year later, to the day—American jets owned by the Mexican military fired missiles over la Ruta Maya.

◎　◎　◎

Late one afternoon, Antonio, K'ayum Ma'ax's father-in-law, ambled by to talk to K'ayum Ma'ax, who was still working on the caoba table, preparing more boards with commercial glue.

Antonio stood tall, barefoot, with long black hair and a tattered tunic. He spoke with few motions. I had seen Antonio on my visit in 1970. He was huddled next to Viejo Chan K'in in the small milpa. I couldn't explain it, but he hadn't aged. Antonio was ashen colored— almost as if he was made of something other than flesh and tunic, some other substance like vine meshed with stony minerals. I recognized him from many years of poring over a video copy of haphazard clips pieced together by my buddy Tomás—our first attempt to edit the film we shot in 1970. All the original film was lost in East Los Angeles where Tomás lived, except that video sample. I also recognized Antonio from several monographs on Lacandón culture in *Geomundo*, as well as Trudi Blom's photos and several studies from Europe. I felt awed—not because he was one of the last

After cutting cane for arrow shafts. Near Lake Nahá, Chiapas. 1970.

of a long line of elders in the village but more because of the way he carried himself, how he talked to K'ayum Ma'ax, and the way he looked at me from a distance. Antonio was very still and yet swayed inside, it seemed, like Lake Ocotal and Lake Nahá, like the trees. I wasn't interested in his knowledge of Lacandón religious matters or even his memories of life in Nahá for the larger portion of this century; nor was I going to inquire into the ways of tropical rain forest agriculture, strategies of thinning that enable a relatively small plot of Lacandón land to yield over seventy different crops. I had made up my mind on the first day that I was here that I wasn't going to butt into anyone's business. I had given up that project. I wasn't here on a "field" query. I was merely here, without much reason other than to visit at best.

Antonio attracted me because I recognized in him something deeper than information and Indian talk—he reminded me of my mother. His softness and his steadiness. His ease and his erect posture. His disregard for sharpness in his attire and in his reflective manner— and yet he possessed something brimming with power that came from years of being aware of what is true. I didn't have the words for this then and I still don't.

K'ayum Ma'ax was different. Even though he kept to himself and had a keen sense of who he was, he was busy, at task, articulate; he was on a mission of sorts. One day he would retaliate, it seemed to me; one day K'ayum Ma'ax would rise up and have the final say about Nahá and its intruders. He would write it and he would carve it as obstinately as he had welded the caoba table with white glue; he would paint it as he had painted for galleries in Palenque and Spain. I sensed this in him and through the various stunted conversations we had. The glued table symbolized this in a way. He was busy mixing opposite and complementary elements, commercial glue and native mahogany; he was improvising a device for the molding of these materials. His house was another example, concrete against grass, cylinder heaters, stoves, stereos, multitrack television against the secrets of the forest; a satellite dish against a hidden shack of arrows behind his house. Antonio was of another order; he walked deeper on the earth.

They both came up to me. K'ayum Ma'ax reminded Antonio about my visit more than two decades ago. Antonio nodded.

"I think I remember you," he told me. "Yes, I remember," he said

"How have you been?"

"Good. I have the flu."

"The flu? Are you going to be all right?"

Antonio pointed to the small mountain behind K'ayum Ma'ax's house. "Just the flu. I am on my way back to the milpa," he said in a small voice.

"How have things been since I was here last time?"

"Good. Colder."

"Colder?"

"Colder. The tobacco won't even grow anymore. The flower blossoms but it gives no seed. A cold wind."

Antonio rubbed his upper arms with his hands. Almost shivering. Dark face, dark lips. He stood a few feet from me.

"And Chan K'in, how is he these days?"

"Good. One hundred twenty years old."

"One hundred and twenty years old?"

"Yes. Me, seventy. Bueno, I will be leaving now."

K'ayum Mario leads the way. Lake Ocotal, Selva Lacandona, Chiapas, 1993.

Back to his milpa in the mountains. He'd come back later in the afternoon. Come back to his house behind the trees where K'ayum Ma'ax whittled wood. I asked him to wait a moment.

"I have something for your flu. Here, take these. Two Theraflu packs. Pour these into hot water and stir, then drink it down. Good for headaches."

Antonio nodded and took the plastic pouches. It was an awkward attempt on my part, maybe because I wanted him to stay a few more minutes, maybe the powder could help. Antonio knew many ways to take care of himself, ways that called upon the sources of the forest, yet he thanked me and waved slightly and left softly, past K'ayum Ma'ax in the backyard, bent with a saw and two long mahogany boards.

⚘ ⚘ ⚘

Last day.
Going up La Ruta with K'ayum Ma'ax.

I've been afraid all along to come and visit the To'ohil, the Great One who knows the words and secrets and stories, the elder teacher of Nahá. I have thought of him for over twenty years, wondering who he is, what he knows, how he has lived. I have wondered about his ways with the earth, the milpas, how he has taken to the logging companies tearing through his village and his lakes. What has he said to his children, what will protect him and his village, who has come to his side? How did he cure the foreigner who fell ill after inquiring about el hombre de la selva?

193

At Na Bolom Trudi Blom's suffering, and the way her words and mind had been snipped back into stumbling syllables, caused me to wonder about el Viejo Chan K'in. When she dies will he die? Are they on a soul track written in by Hachakyüm, the creator of the Lacandones? If the roots of all the trees are tied to the destinies of the stars, how are Viejo Chan K'in and Trudi Blom related?

On one end of the spiral track: Trudi moves into the selva with hands in the mud, with maps and mapmakers, campamentos, clinics, with the magnifying lens of restoration and world alarm, with a self-made fountain for ecological sustenance, for endangered species and peoples, with a tourist museum and dependence trinkets, with capitalism dressed in "progressive" trousers and do-gooder boots. At the other end of the silvery line: Viejo Chan K'in walks. He walks with centuries of conquests and cultural realignments. The traveling men with anteater-noses fall into the milpas with their blue notebooks frozen in their throats. Viejo Chan K'in ambles toward San Cristóbal de las Casas and points to his incense burners and his star cape behind the Na Bolóm display case; he offers balché for the new years ahead. What dreams does he have as the encroaching orb of Tzeltales and cattle grazers, oil engineers and loggers, missionaries and university students stalk his thatched roof and satellite-dish village? I wanted to go through these reflections and dreams with the to'ohil. But I didn't have the words.

K'ayum Ma'ax led me up La Ruta in the morning. Behind la tiendita we scaled the forested slope, turned to the right, and followed a dirt trail. Barking dogs. Sweet smoke in the cool air, moistness under my feet. Outside a large palmita.

"Wait here," K'ayum Ma'ax instructed me.

I was at the entrance to the house made with bajareque walls. My destination: a wide mud, straw and tree-branch house topped with a column of smoke where a pair of thin, sharp dogs stood at the gate. Soon Koh II, one of Viejo Chan K'in's wives, came out, smiled, and with a large gesture of her arms announced that I could enter.

As with Antonio, I had seen her in photographs on Lacandón culture in French, Spanish and German publications. It was as if I had to tear through an elaborate screen of pilfered images and histories that had nothing to do with these people other than to record a vanishing face; they represented a knee-jerk historicism, what global powers do in their spare time—chart explorations and excursions into the wild. Then they pause to take stock of the "primitive," to measure the raw figures against their "advanced" selves. I knew this gesture well; as an American, I was on the verge of becoming an expert at seeking people on the edge of extinction—except in this case I was part of what I was seeking.

For a split second I enjoyed Koh II's welcome, her stern and gallant face, her worn red-striped Ladina dress against the speckled adobe. Her severity and her quick kindness.

As I stepped into the darkness of the house, past the little fire near the entrance where a younger woman and a child turned the embers, as I went forward to the center where K'ayum Ma'ax sat on a tiny chair next to a hanging hammock, I knew that I was entering an ancient and sacred place. Behind the hammock there was a wide bed with many layers of cloth, zarapes. The roof was low and uneven to my eye. The walls seemed moist and speckled with ash.

K'ayum Ma'ax stood up and asked me to take his place on the small chair and moved a few feet behind me. The way was being cleared for me to address Viejo Chan K'in, the house was being rearranged for my visit; each element was being positioned, intricately, yet with great care and ease. Koh II went to the back and sat on a bed against the wall draped with blankets and colored bedsheets.

At the center Viejo Chan K'in was lying deep in his hammock, on his side, facing me. His curled legs were covered by an old tunic, and his arms fell across his body like water. His hands were dark, hard, large, and crooked. I noticed something odd about his hands: They seemed to be frozen, and the fingers were pulled forward, fixed as if clutching an invisible weight, an eternal machete. His face was small and round, brown with eyes that glimmered; his gaze was gentle.

"He came here twenty-three years ago," K'ayum Ma'ax interjected as if to jump-start our conversation. Viejo Chan K'in stretched back, looked up at his son, turned to me, and said something inaudible.

"Yes, I came here about that time," I said as if I was clear about what he had said. "I came with a friend. We landed on a little runway out here by Jorge Paniagua's place. You were at the milpa. We came by cayuco across the lake, with cameras. You were in the milpa with the boys. They were cutting cane for hunting arrows. You were smoking a cigar and laughing with Jorge."

"Yes, I was there. Oh, yes," Viejo Chan K'in said.

"How have you been?"

"The flu . . . it's been cold lately."

"That's what Antonio told me. He says the tobacco doesn't grow anymore."

"It doesn't grow anymore. It's gotten colder. I don't know why."

Viejo Chan K'in mentioned the cold. What was this "cold" they were talking about? Viejo Chan K'in and Antonio were telling me something very direct, and yet I couldn't grasp it.

"I brought some things for you," I said.

I dug into my old turquoise backpack with three Teenage Mutant Ninja Turtles sewn on the back. Pulled out the cigarettes. Koh II screwed her mouth and said that Viejo Chan K'in couldn't smoke now. I gave her the large cigarette cartons with a few packs missing. Nelly Maldonado had told me that Chan K'in loved mayonnaise; I brought the jar out. I had bought it at a supermercado next to the zócalo in San Cristóbal. Viejo Chan K'in smiled. This is his favorite, Koh II said. I found the Christmas rum cakes wrapped in airtight silver packages. A good choice—I could tell by Koh II's approving smile.

One of the thin dogs came in and sniffed at the embers by the small bright-haired boy near the entrance. The child had white skin and white hair. I lost the little balance I had achieved. He was the same boy who accompanied Leo, the man with the Travel All van, at Lake Nahá a few days ago. I hadn't realized that he was one of Chan K'in's youngest children. The canvas sack of granola that my friend Jorge Herrera gave me in San Francisco was the best gift. Organic fiber with almonds and dates, raisins, and honeyed oats. K'ayum Ma'ax almost jumped up with excitement. He exclaimed to Koh II that this was what his father needed for his grippe. Viejo Chan K'in nodded his head and smiled. We spoke a few more words.

"Have you seen Trudi?" he asked me.

"Yes, I've been staying at Na Bolom."

"How is she?"

"She's not too well."

"Oh, not well."

"She can't talk anymore."

"Ah."

"She doesn't walk well."

"Ah."

Viejo Chan K'in's eyes sparkled and receded into another time. His frail body moved an inch or two to adjust his posture; he rubbed his hands and fell deeper into his hammock and looked away for a moment, coughed. Our meeting had come to a close.

"Well, I just wanted to come by and visit you," I told him. "Your son K'ayum Ma'ax has been very hospitable. I am leaving him an old movie about the days when I came here the first time. For you— thank you, Chan K'in, I just wanted to thank you. For everything."

I said farewell to Viejo Chan K'in and Koh II and walked back to La Ruta with K'ayum Ma'ax. Silent through the reeds and grasses. Tears began to well up in my eyes. Down the slope to the open gravel by the tiendita.

My things were already packed from the night before. It was an old habit from always living on the move. My wanderings as a child, alone with my mother, came to me again. My father's absences, his disappearance into the night, into his other family in New Mexico, my aloneness turned into a knot in my throat as I double-checked the few bags in my room. My keen ability to survive on sparse supplies and in almost any environment, my poet-on-the-run preparedness, had something to do with my early and fast and lonesome years as a child.

Visiting Viejo Chan K'in was a culminating point. Even though we spoke about very little, I felt that I had been filled with a set of truths too big to hold or articulate. My chest was tight as I walked over to K'ayum Ma'ax's wife, Nuk, and thanked her for everything. She asked me to stay and then gave me a red bean necklace. I thanked K'ayum Ma'ax who had by now put on an indigo blue cardigan over his tunic. He looked more serious with the sweater, more distant.

By noon I stood at the edge of La Ruta, with my bags on the road, waiting for the Tumbo to take me back to the beginning.

From *Mayan Drifter: Chicano Poet in the Lowlands of America,* 1997. Revised.

Chan K'in Viejo. Selva Lacandona, Chiapas, 1970.

Indocumentos
(een-doh-koo-mehn-tohs) /
Undocuments / noun:

AZTLÁN CHRONICLES, VOL. 9, NO. 9

- *Multi-vocal passage-ware lacking authorized verifications regarding entry and/or social identity.*
- *Texts utilized by non-state-actors for mobile existence in-between officialized national entities.*
- *A system of undocumented signification of & for the people.*
- *The spoken subject within the context of exile, illegal ID status and/or "alien" assignations.*
- *Transgressive acts of perception and interpretation within a shifting borderlands territory.*
- *Flux moments in-between being & non-being.*

Thinking if Mexican@s & Latin@s have been historically cast in one way or another as "illegals," & "undocumented" entities whether through "soft" cultural border-patrol work such as most official media narratives & the "footing" of most political & electoral platforms or the "hard" classifications of foreign & international policy, structured force & military surveillance, then the word & texts of such actors, regardless of their citizenship must be "undocumented" as well. For the people, the text becomes Floricanto, at the hands of a borderizing society, the word is not a document of song, soul & witness at all; it is an undocument lacking authority, self, place, voice, meaning,

position, orientation, structure, body, connection, his-
tory, trajectory, time, power, space & most of all—a field
of & for social consciousness. In the Floricanto trek, you
embrace the undocumented—blurred open-jacket strutters
through the void of slippage & scattered phenomena, with
undocuments swishin' out from their purses, pockets, shoes,
& our hungry impossible mouths

HOW TO BE A WARRIOR
IN THE AZTLÁN LIBERATION ARMY
4 ACTOS

Circa 1967–2006

HOW TO BE A WARRIOR
FOR THE AZTLÁN
LIBERATION ARMY

Didn't have the eight-track

but I had the rest—

Three Roses pomade, stiff khakis, greased head, Levis as hard as
ceramic pants, cardboard boxes instead of suitcases (even when I
went to the university orientation), a penchant for tragedies,
especially those performed by Pedro Infante in *Nosotros los pobres* or
Buñuel's *Los olvidados*, was in love with Sarita Montiel, the Spanish
actress who starred in *La violetera*, wanted the long honey of her
reddish hair pouring down her back & María Victoria, her manly
voice and fish-shaped black steel dress, ate biznagas for breakfast,
roasted chicken feet with cocido for dinner as I gawked at Lawrence
Welk with my mom, wore navy blue beanies and navy blue turtlenecks
to high school thinking I was a Post-Chicano Beatnik, even though I
was the only one who thought that, sometimes I would wear my Day-
Glo green short sleeve & my tight silver-lined black hustler sport coat
bought on pawnshop row, Fifth Street, San Diego (for junior high
graduation). Still wear it. For lonche, in the early years—tomate and
butter sanwishes or sanwishes de sardina with a tiny green and yellow
can of pineapple juice (me & George Escalera were the only
Chicanos at Lowell Elementary who carried giant chrome can
openers), these days I make the best Chicano antipasto: sardinas

coloradas either in mustard sauce or tomates with French bread, diced jalapeños, cilantro and relish, tastes like the Vietnamese tortas they make in Sanjo, in Little Saigon. Every Halloween I smeared my face with brown oil, made big holes on my clothes so I could look like a pirate or a hobo, the only roles I knew how to play and the cheapest, wait a minute, I did have a radio, a twelve-transistor box that I took to Mission Beach in San Diego with Heredia, scouting for chavalas & his famous primo Hugo said he knew about French Lit. Always wore flattops, Mohawks, or butches, now it doesn't matter, 'cuz my head actually is square, my stepchildren laugh at it, I feel good about those ondas, there's more too, like when I used to raise my head during the Pledge of Allegiance, in first grade—Central Elementary because I had questions & when I sang tenor in high school in a barbershop quartet, puffed shirts with garters on the upper sleeves, this is how I made myself speak out, how I waxed my soul, in this style, put a teatro together in '70, a Puerto Rican wrapped up in aluminum foil supposed to represent nuestra opresión, then Troka, a conga group from Fresno, in '82 spent thousands to make it to Boston where we sang a Dion piece at MIT as an encore. For a couple of years walked around sin calzones, in manta pants, huaraches, or thongs, drinking purified water, carried in a small glass jar—tied to my turquoise belt, the one from Veracruz, I was on a search, my heart was open, talking about El Movimiento, using the words *espíritu* & *liberation*, ask my camaradas, they know and who knows what I'll do next.

From *Notebooks of a Chile Verde Smuggler*, 2004.

LA LLORONA POWER-WOMAN CONFIDENTIAL

Classified Sheet: La Llorona Meets Dr. Espanto.

Des E. Torny-Yadda is one of her secret identities: a short, dark brunette with thick glasses, a mole on her left cheek and a knock-kneed gait. Family from East Juárez, Chihuahua. Jumped the border illegally and took up residence in El Paso, Texas. Graduated from Jefferson High and went on to UCLA; paid her way by selling Mayan herbal hangover lotions to the Greek frats by Hedrick Hall.

Des E. is a human mask, a useful day-to-day moniker in the big city haze of mauve-colored offices, stiletto acquaintances, and smog-squeezed personas. On a clear day you can flip your head back, gaze up, and count most of the thirty stories of the Barrel Linch TransAmerican Tower in the financial district of San Francisco. She now works as a broker on floor 27: International Investments. Her male Latino colleagues call her *desatornillada*, "screwy, crazy sellout" or Des for short. Envy, cold stares and menudo-smelling blazers do not faze DTY. Old macho dogs caught in a downward career spiral, these she gobbles with a Granola bar and washes them down with a half a cup of 2% fat milk as she downloads trade data from ITT and Microsoft.

"TY" is what her white coworkers call her when they see her stepping out to a Coho Salmon Cappuccino brunch with Dr. Espanto Esparza, the highest-paid VP in the business.

"TY's got what it takes—brains, brains and more brains," they say biting their glossy fingernails, praying for a break.

What the junior brokers don't know is that by night TY takes on another ID. She presses the computer code at the gray marble entrance door in the private parking lot, slides up the elevator and swishes back into Espanto's terminal where she swings through the global files of Barrel Linch, milking accounts in Switzerland into guerrilla files on the Nicaraguan coast, undoing New York diamond notes and dropping them into the Underground Indian and Peasant Front on the border between Chiapas and Yucatán.

They call her "La Llorona" because, as the Indians say, "She has come back to save her children." In fact, "La Llorona" is her code name on the Internet; she appears and disappears in a keystroke. Bank of America, Banco Serfín, Banamex, Sumitomo, Maritime Arctic Bank of Commerce; they have all been gouged and bitten by the shadowy electric hand of "La Llorona." It is reported that Des E.'s current project is to hit W.H.A.T., otherwise know as W. Hey All Houser Timber Incorporated, in Seattle. A note was found in their quarterly Board of Directors agenda: "Eliminate environmental disaster, save the spotted owls and the last great redwoods or I'll bite your heads off!"

Today Dr. Espanto noticed that his Van Gogh screen saver was jittery, the mouse pad upside down—there definitely was something wrong. His Virgen de Guadalupe frame was turned backward. Espanto's family album of three, Shannon, his wife, Erin and Espantito, the cross-eyed baby, was crooked as if someone had pulled the photos and then replaced them in a hurry. Breathing hard, he turned to get a cup of caffeine from his espresso machine and saw the brief letter, a print-out, addressed to him:

Dr. Espanto:

You've got exactly seven hours and seven minutes to change the fate of the world. And I am going to see that Destiny moves kindly. First of all, you must do the following (or boo-hoo: you may watch your family fotos on the next *America's Most Wanted* TV show, brought to you by the FBI computer files):

uno: Deposit all the Washington, DC, presidential lobby accounts into the #12 Vata-Chiapas file;
dos: Pentagon and NASA budget investments in earthmovers, hydroelectric power loans, and environmental clean-up accounts move to #441 Chava-Rwanda account;
tres: Promote all the women on your staff, immediately, or I'll bite your head off!
La Llorona

Dr. Espanto filled his Vesuvio cup with a double espresso, sat down, and stared into a Chinatown shrunken into a tiny green square down below. He took a bite from an old custard empanada pastry his mother had left him four months ago, on Father's Day. A funny taste radiated through his mouth, a musky air came up to his nostrils. As he crouched over his monitor and followed "La Llorona's" instructions, he sniffed again. The perfume was familiar. "Des E. Torny-Yadda wears this brand, *Z-Latina*—a fancy new rain forest musk made out of tropical grasses," Espanto whispered as he deleted the transactions. He would wait for the night; Dr. Espanto screwed his eyes. In a New Age mask, one of those gray clear gels—with a red bandanna and a black hat, he would peer behind his office door. Things were about to change fast. "Just wait, baby," he laughed to himself with a new air of confidence, "tomorrow, in the *Daily Salsa Examiner*, in bold letters, the headline is gonna read: Mystery Masked Man Saves Nation. Latina Culprit Captured by Exec!"

To be continued—

"La Llorona's Last Tear"
or
"Will 'Lowrider Sally Chingas' Rescue
Her Old Sidekick from Jefferson High and Save the Day?"

From *Notebooks of a Chile Verde Smuggler*, 2004.

EVER SPLIT YOUR PANTALONES WHILE TRYING TO LOOK CHINGÓN?

For all hard-core Chicano lawyers who have never
admitted to anyone that they are ex-altar boys.

Like when I was coming back from a Santana Blues Band Concert at
the Fillmore, back in '67—this guy with a Led Zeppelin black leather
jacket laid a pastrami & mota barf on my back, like, like when I was
serving misa de gallo at our Lady of Guadalupe on Kearny Street in
'61 and Padrecito Benjamín was raising the Host for benediction
("Watch his hand," they told me) and I had to ring the bell with my
right hand just like the altar boy champion José Mendieta, but I was
left-handed so I rang it with my right hand and it sounded like
guacamole, like, like when I first met Margie, took her to the Hungry
Tiger in North Beach and we danced, had cannelloni, came back to
visit my buddies Demarest and Alvarez and Eva L. (Demarest's novia)
who made tons of pilipino refin and wanting to impress Eva &
Margie, I wolfed the pancit, washed it down with smokes & two tall
glasses of rum that I thought were Coca-Cola and barfed on the red
carpet with music note designs on them as I broke over the leather
armchair like that, or like in '58 when we went to Tijuana & I was
wearing the wool, Mexicano double-breasted suit that my tío
Fernando wanted me to wear to the cine Bujazán to watch *La momia
azteca* until I was sweating so hard that when I touched the metal seat

211

in front of me during a María Félix kiss, I electrocuted myself, screamed so loud they turned the houselights on, everyone thought I was dying, like this, like when I burned my mustache off trying to blow out my birthday kequi or like when I stood up at St. Anthony's and my pantalones had eaten themselves into my cuchi-cuchi and everyone in the back rows, especially Doña Aguado, La Católica, looked at it. Like that.

From *Notebooks of a Chile Verde Smuggler*, 2004.

RICARDO "SLICK RIC" SALINAS (Rappin' at the 24th Street Fair, S.F.)

—'til the wheels fall off.

You look so slick in your hot lemon parachute pants
and your cut-off tank, dude,

de aquellas
& Dominique doing her spin on the staging.
I remember

when you were writing love letters to her
and I had Margie's photo on the wall back
in the sugarshack on the hill

when we were doing Teatro
for Luis Valdez. Shiiiit, the wall
looked like some kind of 1969
North Beach poster shop.

But, they closed them down
and the Teatro season is over
(except for Herb, he just got a gig
with Teatro Esperanza, right?).

It's not a Movement anymore, carnal.
Not really a street fair either.
It's something else.

You know what Slick?
I got a feeling your rap got through
the cut on the great wall
where despair set in long ago.

From *Facegames*, 1987.

On Tour, 1992

AZTLÁN CHRONICLES, VOL. 2, NO. 13

When I toured with Amiri Baraka in '92 after both of us
received an award from the Intersection for the Arts in
San Francisco I noticed how Baraka moved & sang & ignited
at every podium whether we had six people in the audience
like in Buffalo, New York, or whether we had a cool hep
group lined up all the way to the back like in the Big
Apple at St. Mark's or whether we had a dark hot smoky
cauldron of witnesses ready to spark up into new beings
ready to inquire into every syllable offered in the midst
of rebellion burning streets neighborhoods & riot syrup
cityscapes like in Los Angeles days after the Rodney King
explosion

RODNEY KING, THE BLACK CHRIST OF LOS ANGELES & ALL OUR WHITE SINS

1992

RODNEY KING, THE BLACK CHRIST OF LOS ANGELES & ALL OUR WHITE SINS

Late April, early May 1992, first read at
Beyond Baroque, Venice, California.

Listening to Santana, again.
The verdict came down. Four white cops
—found not guilty.

Rodney went down for all of us.
This alley guitar pours its juice into my veins.

His jawbone moved, he spoke
the words of our origin, our names.

The blue-black nightsticks came down
to his plump flesh, across the face, the bones inside.
The bones wavered into the heart
and they exploded for us,

I am kneeling down.

In East Los, La Raza is contemplating Cinco de Mayo
and the French skin that still covers our nakedness.

219

A cloud with the face of W. E. B. Du Bois hangs
over the Sherwin Williams paint store

in South Central L.A.—
W. E. B. said the crisis of the twentieth century
would be the color line.

Churn up more blackness through the windows.
Two Chicanas run out of a busted mall, one loaded
with bags of Pampers,
the other with loaves of bread.

Beneath the Harbor Freeway bridge, a tired man
who looks like Ho Chi Minh spits
at the fire trucks going by.

The vapor of kerosene comes up from the apartments
and *chile piquín* peppers on the black asphalt grill.

Streets smell like Guadalajara
where there is a giant crutch being built by the *políticos*.

They are chanting
la tierra mojada—

"The earth has the aroma of rain," they say.
That's what they sing at the mariachi festivals.

This is the *colonia* that blew up a few weeks ago.
Pemex let the gasoline burst underground. Said

it was too expensive to fix the line leaks.

So, they let gas run beneath
the bedroom floors of the Mexicans

—oil and gasoline.

These are the psychic sheets
of our penitence and liberation.

A Harley
—on fire

at the Martin Luther King Boulevard intersection
a few blocks from the Sports Arena. A blonde

woman in jeans—pushed out of her Toyota pickup,
a reddish '84. The Harley is melting

into a chrome praying mantis. Crackle and spit.
Hundreds of oblong bodies rush.

My cousin Vincent
who spent twenty years in the pen sits on his beat-up sofa,
laughs at the blue flash in the corner of his living room.

He picks his nose,
sneers at the newswoman who is beginning
to stumble on the TelePrompTer.

More choppers and tanks.
Tomorrow is paycheck day.

La lana,
la piola,
la rifa,
el cartón,
la feria,

except this time
la gente will cash their welfare checks in a chopper.

Or a National Guard tank,
just maybe.

I am behaving like a Mexican,
the kind you see in Cheech and Chong movies.

The post offices are down
and the banks in San Bernardino are down.

Longo is going up in flames too.
Money is worth a bowl of beans today.

The supermarkets are open, everything is free.
Ginsberg was wrong about the supermarket

—Whitman
and Lorca are elsewhere.

This is my atonement,
this is my resurrection,
this is the way of the black cross,
the brown crown of thorns.

The liquor stores are ours. The laundries are ours.
Shirts we never wore are finally pressed, ready
for church, and the toasters
with extra-wide slots are ours too.

There is a pearl-white Mercedes being kicked in
by six kids with Adidas and torn faces.

A bloodied Chicano is taking potshots
at my neighbor, Taiji, as he swerves
into an on-ramp going west. The Guard
is on the way, the *federales* are on the way.

A cop shoots mace into a white boy's eyes
—how does it feel, how does it?

Another guy fondles his own breasts
as he looks at a VCR behind the window.
A pack of Michelob,
a gold suit and a helmet,
badges

and justice
and ratchets.

Sirens come for Rodney's spirit. Someone gets run over,
the legs are crushed on Normandie Avenue—

a young vato's brains slide down
the headrest of his '59 Biscayne;

on the way back from a soccer game
he met a bullet with his name.

Rodney has answered all the silences.
It is a tender voice, a cavernous tenderness.

Greenish smoke curls toward Hollywood Boulevard
Edward James Olmos comes out to clean up with brooms.

There is a crew of white students
huddled in a hamburger diner called Burgertime,
they are saying—

Blacks and minorities got their share already
"Why are they doing this?"

"Why?" they say,

and another newscaster uses the word *animal*
as he peeks through the tube.

and Rodney's white lawyer's face stretches
as he becomes black in an uncanny way.
He is looking for more words about justice.

There is no Black Christ.

I said it to get myself going. I was loaded
with stupor and complacency. Because
I live in the suburbs of North Fresno.
Because I see fat tractors and rigs

smooth the ground
for more cells of silence.

Now, I have spilled my guts
in a Mexican way

Need more fuel now;
thought I was clean. Thought I could do

with the other things,
but I need the fuel now, need the cheap kind.

My wife Margarita is upstairs taking a shower.
The water is churning through the ceiling
making high-pitched sounds,
shredding sounds.

More smoke. Another line of dead,

nameless dead with one name for all of them.
Maybe our name, maybe

it is my name and your name they are calling.

An old woman in an oversized sweater,
in denims, drinks
a hot Gatorade from the mess of a 7-Eleven.
A Korean vato and a Mexican dude
are fingering their mouths

—their stores are in ashes. These are the ashes.
Cross your foreheads on this Ash Friday,

this Ash Saturday of black palms
and talkative gutters full of rainbow juice,
the kind that comes from radiators, skulls,
cracked batteries.

This year we had a long Easter.
It got caught up in a bad cycle of drought,
earthquakes, blood, glue,
and pregnant cats and bird nests thrown open
by a car crash.
The broken birds are soapy without skin,

there is a tiny purple ball still
ticking inside their stomachs;

the beaks are too yellow
—the color of emergency plastic tape,
the type cops put around a murder scene.
Don't step on them, if there is anything you do
—please don't step on them.

At Union Square, in San Francisco,
they are ripping down the neon signs,
right across from the St. Francis Hotel. My mother
worked there as a salad girl in the forties,
right after the war;

that's when Lawrence Welk was the main feature
on weekends, and they are on Market Street too
by the Embassy Theater
where you can see a porno show for one dollar.

I am carrying a triple landscape in my head.
Walking around with tears on my ragged face.
Congas and timbales by the trashcans.

I can see everything—San Francisco,
Guadalajara, and the city which was an empire
once upon a time. I used to go there
as a kid and look at my hands to make sure
I was there—
to remember myself there
by the shape of my hands.

This is the way of the Gods in the Streets,
this is the Gospel of Rodney King,
the Black and Brown Wand of Inspiration.

From *Night Train to Tuxlta*, 1994.

227

In Gold-Leaf Trungpa Seed

AZTLÁN CHRONICLES, VOL. 4, NO. 30

Last night talking with my partner, Margarita, I asked
her, "Am I caught up with the past?" Yes, she said & then,
as usual, she remained still. The past—or—the future. Can
they be interchangeable? What lies in the present then?
Nostalgia is a form of aggression, Chogyam Trungpa Rin-
poche, the Tibetan wise poet, says. Years ago I learned
this lesson after it cost me all the editons of a poetry
book that had just been published. After visiting the
Shambhala Mountain Meditation Center on April 21, a clean
& clear Saturday, after driving up from Naropa University
in Boulder, Colorado, with Valentín, about twenty-three
years old, a free man who lives there, & taking a few steps
into the center of the mountains, at the core of the vil-
lage, between forests, shrines & bear tracks & gazing
quickly at the landscape, & the Stupa where the Buddha
sits in gold leaf Trungpa seed, I noticed a glaze of light
shimmering over the material of the slender hills &
makeshift huts, on the short oxygen itself, caught a tiny
shard of the present that remains forever. We call it the
present, but it is not the present

AUTOBIOGRAPHY OF A CHICANO TEEN POET

Circa 1982-1988

AUTOBIOGRAPHY OF A CHICANO TEEN POET

For Rosita, RIP, Alvinita & Chente & Tito &
Julie & Chelita & Yooyee & Beto Jr. & Ray G.

I am a downtown boy, handcuffed
when I was eleven
for being accomplice to armed robbery.

I speak shoeshine parlor brown and serve
as the only usher in *Club Sufrimiento 2001.*

You can call me Johnny B. Nice.

Tender hollow-eyed whores and
busted novelists in spiderweb trenchcoats
are partners in the law firm where I live.

Thelonious Monk,
Janis Joplin, sip with me when you can.
I am out here playing my blues,
my autobiography of penny arcade rendezvous.

From here I can see the Mayor.
He just got three years probation for perjury
and now he's working for the "homeless."
Who was he working for in the first place?

I used to go to church, but the wind-up doll got tired
and couldn't speak proper English anymore.
So, God punished it and drove it into the wilderness
where it found a color film of a Wonderkid
selling Language and Infinity to the lost on Inferno Street.
But, the translation wasn't bilingual, even though
they showed it at the Casino with a triple porno movie.

My brother died in the ring,
stabbed 14 times by the King of Desire.
All the electric guitars moaned in the pawnshops
and my mother grew smaller with memory.

Above me,
the phosphor light coughs and sweats.

I can't wait to see the red-striped cellophane
from cigarette packs—whirl
into a fire at the center of the street.

From *Facegames*, 1987.

STORY &
KING BLVD
Teen-age Totems

Skirt fenders on a two-tone Plymouth like the one my uncle Ferni drove to Mexico City back in '57. At night the street looks like Xmas. Angelina ran away from the shelter. Her foster mother wants to keep her, but she lost her license. She got caught with cocaine, the kids said. Angie's boyfriend used to bring it over. Now, this is hearsay, okay? He got stabbed last week. He said he was going to support her. I used to want to be a singer. Her grandfather did things to her for years. She just met her brother who's 19 years old. They told me he was my uncle. I hate social workers, why don't they leave me alone. You have to turn yourself in to the shelter, Angie. Maybe when I have my baby, my mom will be happy. I know she will. And we'll talk and she'll take care of me. I hate her. She misses you. She hits my sister all the time. She says it's okay to go out, but, when I come home she calls me a slut. The counselor is looking for your file. But, I am going to have my baby, anytime, now. What are you going to name him, her? It's going to be a boy. Anthony, or maybe, Carlos. She manipulates you, she knows the system. She can't have her way. She's still underage. 14. Tell her I have a satellite home for her. As of now, I have a warrant on her. I used to want to be a singer. Who's that girl at the bus stop. It's midnight.

From *Facegames*, 1987.

BABY BLUE

For Roberto Bedoya.

He wrote an article about KJ in high school and got a good grade. He knew what he was talking about. Janie was glad. I think she was the only one he trusted, maybe. Anyway, the dude strolled in and said check out my paper, Janie. Everybody likes it. Not bad, huh. Janie looked at him. She didn't ask him what's 37 plus 23? To see if he could handle it. Mr. Lara at the center would have done that. I know you are still using, Cricket. Don't try to hold him down. Get the furniture out of the way. Dim the lights. Talk to him. If he starts going off on something, tell him, Hey Cricket, look at what you done to your shirt, man, now what are you going to wear to school? Bring him home. The blue tunnel, man, see? There. Man! When he starts talking about it, get to him. Say anything. Get him to react. Don't let him in. He may never come back. If he's on the floor and starts getting stiff and foam comes up from his mouth, pull out your wallet or a belt or something so he won't bite his tongue in half. If it's you & KJ is what's happening because it's live or because you can take it, don't bullshit yourself, don't write about it, drop it.

Ernie takes studio art.
That's pretty good for a 10th grader.
Everything here is new to him. He's a very intense boy.
Right now, he's working on a life-size sculpture
made out of fiber strands and resin.

A tall male figure
in flames.

Floating in a tank
Trying to scream.

He's buried
wrapped in a gauze of little fingers pointing at him.

From *Facegames*, 1987.

Painted Rubber Doll

AZTLAN CHRONICLES, VOL. 3, NO. 4

My first installation was a blackish painted rubber doll I
did in '66 purchased on D Street San Diego at a second-
hand store the best kinda store for artists so there I was
pouring varnish mixed with red oil paints nailed it to an
enamel painted white wooden cross one two three go go go
that's all I sat there in my art studio class at San Diego
High with my *Autobiography of Malcolm X* in my hand &
somekind of sociology book on race breathe breathe ahhhh
Mrs. Steiger my art teacher said I am behind you whatever
happens as faculty & students circled me & the cross at
the first exhibit yeah that's how I started out as a
painter & installation dude since then it's always been
about painting everything laying down a new palette knife
a funny odd pouring pressing of Matisse green faces
Siqueiros metropolis dumpster orphans Kahlo self-painted
body casts then there's the painters that paint without us
or the others without ideas or views in particular
painters that are merely brushes themselves only laughing
breathing in out in out falling rising in space

CALIFAS NORTE

Circa 1976-1986

CALIFAS NORTE
Juanalicia Finishing Her Mural at the S.F. Mime Troupe's Headquarters (the old Fantasy Records Bldg.), 1985

For the cast, Juanalicia and all the mural squadrons of the Américas.

Lenny Bruce,
dressed in harlequin overalls flamingo pink &
Chinatown jade, is on center stage.

At the top
near the serpent flames, the stage lights and the *placazo*

CALIFAS NORTE
VIVA LA RAZA

meet the Dragon Lady of the Nuclear Metropolis
& the MC for the Hypodermic Club giving you
that Dale Gas smile: Come on Honey, anything
shoe-wanna
kiss-kiss for the Birth of the New Baby from Babylon!

And now,
Ladies & Gentlemen, presenting
the Fascist Tenor, the one and only, Dictator Marcos
performed by Melesio Magdaluyo

(and for back-up, Chumley playing Pinochet and
Mobutu doing the flex-strut).

Juana says Melesio has round resonant features
as if he was made out of chocolate and violin.

Eddy Robledo is in the background,
a guerrillero, preparing, near a campfire
looking South over San José, el Río Usumacinta,
San Cristóbal de las Casas, San Pedro de los Lagos,
el Río Lempa, through the Matto Grosso
to Antofagasta.

Factwino is my hero!

He's on the door that leads to the rehearsal room
with his arms open, so that when you go in
he gets you with his hands

Plak!
Plak!

He knows everything
like how much Exxon and Kodak invest in South Afrika
or how many years you have left to live after working

in the Tin Mines of Bolivia or

the height of the Parabola of Rape in the city.
So, what you gonna do?

He's you when you're no longer drowsy.
Zas!

(Shabka has been doing Factwino with Joaquín Aranda
for so long that he's sounding Shakespearean.)

There is no escape! Because

My man Cal Tjader is playing *Ritmo Caliente*
at the Black Hawk riffin'
like when cousin Tito used to come home late,
wake us up and shine the flashlight into our eyes
on Harrison Street.

(Chente and I would squint at the Horace Silver Quintet
and Dave Brubeck Quartet album covers on the wall and hear
everything in our third grade heads all over again!)

Mongo Santamaría, slap your hands. La liberación tiene sabor
a guanábana, guayava y papaya. Ask anyone around here
for more info on the theory.

Sabor
Calor
Jugo

Amor
Color
Rebozo
Rainbow
Soul

¡Adentro!

Caribbean *mole* skin conga splash mambo tumbáo & Paul
Desmond is tapping his left blue suede shoe
melting sax
vermilion blues spilling maraca *zandunga* jazz
heat on Treat Street spinning the scaffolding
and Juanalicia's sketches into the air.

All the Latino busboys & meseras & motel maids
& the Mexican Chef at the St. Francis are throwing
a molotov strike for better wages all the way
from Nob hill, Embarcadero through Lombard Street
to the waterfront!

Rising
brazo a brazo.

Watch out!

A payasa
with a red star on her forehead
is looking at your face. Right Now!

Emmanuel is in the audience
(he and Juanalicia just got married)
and Doña Josefina with her pineapple hat,
look

there's Musiki on the ivories popping a sixteenth note
over Dolores Park while Joan Holden types out another
draft for the next show of
diamonds

in Audrey's eyes as she tap dances with Sharon & Wilma Bonét
the butterfly
on Stevie Oropeza's manta pants & María Acosta
flying
campesina de Centro América es el Volcan de la Justicia
in the Misión Varrio above

in the 3rd quarter of the dawn
the City Hall Hyena
lipsyncs

one for the money
two for the show
three to get ready
now, let's go to war!
La bomba tiene una lengua administrativa
su-ave. Comprendee? *¡Peligro!*

Everything is alive,

this tropical theatre
Carpa de la Gente
where
Firulais is home
with *La Vitola* & Stepin Fetchit,
El Mantequilla
and *Cantínflas* wearing a Zoot Suit Cholo Punk
Mohawk
Rocker double proper
Chileno
Tex-Mex
in
a Califas glow
esperanza
fire
opal

raining spirit shafts;
a teenager named Desire catching a Muni to Freedom
an *abuelita* called *Vida Libre Para Mis Hijos*
carrying our words into wise rebel güagüancó revelation.

pinturaltura
from your hands into the Earth
soaring
through our eyes.

From *Facegames*, 1987.

MEXICAN WORLD MURAL / 5 x 25

In memory of Ramón Medina Silva from El Colorín, Huichol Nation.

In August he boarded the bus/the A.D.O./for southern México and
saw the hunched posts/those gray tree posts/one Emiliano Zapata
one woman with contraband rifles/orphans in uniforms of fury
against the sugarcane growers of Anenecuilco/stopping time and its
veins the year 1914 coughed in the splinters/behind the rocks his
horse in green mourning was scratching the dust of commanders/in
Iguala/the moon full of huipiles of blood and rust/bitten
cartridges/you saw him in the darkness of throatless generals/their
torn muslin undershirts purple with the rage of lizards/but you
didn't want to talk to him/I knew you were an old woman with small
dark hands/he knew you would never come back to see me/you
never wanted troops/you wanted something on your breasts/some
torn-out light/for your house for your children an eternal seed in the
joints/of those withered gardens you pointed toward Morelos/that
highway/where Lucio Cabañas denounced the soldiers' grins/with
centuries of fever in the eyes that gave you life/so alone/why?/what
are you doing on this barren land?/the bus is full of sand the
suitcases drowning in ants/the soldiers brought us some papers and
told us that in México there was hope they made us/cross ourselves
they ordered us into a single file/toward a gold hotel full of
architects in robes designing/the wallet of stars and/you followed us I
wanted to touch you/your shoulders were whispering/you took me to

your mountain house/of missions and tin slums and you open your
hands and I look into the abyss/the smoke/the president's rattler
and the infinite flame in the bones of your/children

From *Akrílica*, 1989.
Translated from the Spanish by Stephen Kessler, Magaly Fernández,
Sesshu Foster and Dolores Bravo.

EVENING PORTRAIT OF AN EL PASO, TEXAS HERO—ROBERTO "VAY" MELENDEZ

He was just one of us, but a hero.
I mean not in a big way but real,
because he was one of us.
Simon Ortiz, from "What I Mean," *Woven Stone*

I was at the front
the first ones
It was '66—from El Paso, Texas
the other Marines who came after us
got their names on the plaque
thass what everyone talks about
'68
'69
'70
no one mentions '66
go to the Veterans' Building you'll see what I mean
we got nothing see this tag on my hat
what year does it say?
'66 thass right

we were the first ones out there
whatever was in front of us

came down—women children men cows
then we torched the village
we made the road for the rest to follow
every day
every night
Melendez the officers called out
Melendez is crazy
Let Melendez burn out first they laughed
I mean I volunteered for everything
and you know what
after a while I began to love it
It happened like that

when it was over I told the commander
I wanted a six-month extension
there I was alone
with him in the room
no he said no Melendez
you are sick in the head

so I came back home
no one knew where I was
but there in a gown
in the hospital man I was
on thorazine all those drugs
you name it
I was on it
you don't know how it feels
in here
inside the chest

all those lives
never go away
they burn they burn

I want you to write my story
but you are gonna have to
catch me on a good day
and I am not going to talk about
all that chicano grunt shit yeah it was there
so what so what
gonna tell you what really happened
I look at Melendez
my brother-in-law
water comes down from his eyes
a week before Thanksgiving 2006
we are in the kitchen
his wife Yoli leans on the velvet sofa
stares somewhere away
from the bluish light
as if a cloud in the wind an eye
the grandchildren play
Ultimate Wrestling men
in a cage

Melendez notices his daughter Rose
open the refrigerator for a beer
for her husband policeman from Colton
and Savanna and Jennifer the granddaughters
chase each other up the beige stairs
I am their hero

that is all he says rubs his cheek
the Box Spring mountains darken
nine miles north of the house
on Revelation Way

New work

En Route from Honduras to San Francisco

AZTLÁN CHRONICLES, VOL. 7, NO. 38

Dunno how I really got that wild crazy furry edge of a one-
bedroom apartment on Capp Street 24th Street one block
north the perfect pad for a poet with a penchant for French
bread cream soda Italian sardines olives pesto gorgonzola
panaderías blowin' the flavors all the way from Alabama
Street right in there where me & my cousin Chente deliv-
ered tortillas in '58 right across from the York Theater
we'd go on Saturdays to gawk at each other jumping sweaty
tormented faces turning into lampshades & all kinda shapes
so so I was back had just rolled back from San Diego in
'77 to the Mission District in '78 me & Pancho Alarcón said
we were going to take over the City the poetry scene so so
we hooked up with Murguía & his cadre with Hirschman & his
cadre & then it all came to a dead stop or was it a begin-
ning the revolution in Nicaragua the revolution in El
Salvador where I had been in '74 boppin' around in love
unshaven rough & hungry complex catching a new idea the
apartment was #10 windows over Capp Street typing on Alar-
cón's Olivetti or on my Selectric which I had bought with
an NEA check in '79 the door opened in '81 & in walked
Philippe from Honduras with a stash of fotos of the dis-
placed the bombed the shattered campesinos bitten by La
Guardia Nacional in Las Cabañas El Salvador swimming fast
across Río Lempa pitiful & powerful at the same time the
mothers breast-feeding the fathers' eyes lost the children
like twigs & mad jazz sticks scattered on the tobacco-col-
ored soil with tarps & cans & cigarettes & hope & sadness

all over those gaunt hills of Honduras here here Philippe
said these are their poems see how they write about the
oppressor as the pharaoh see that see that he said & we
jammed all night & I took those photos & I took those sto-
ries made of rivers bodies muddy smeared raggedness
scuffed auroras

EARTH CHORUS

Circa 1981-1983

EARTH CHORUS

For the campesinos of Las Cabañas, a municipality of El Salvador,
and for Philippe Bourgois.

It is the earth that snarls & slashes with black jaguar eyes & teeth &
incandescent claws the Pharaoh & his troops of delicate overcoat &
medal delight it is the earth that reveals lies & recognizes with lightning
& birds & bare feet & adolescent brows & cheekbones of lava the
Traitor & his wire hands & plantation laws & slave labor it is the earth
flowing with the dew of brave women & men on march with rivers &
coffee plantations with salt & fury it is the earth that determines the
new furrows the knives of plants of shining flesh the skin rising the
viper of rhymes & the guerilla war breathing fire extinguishing the
plague the silk web the false tower it is the earth that hurls red whips &
elastic bodies infinite fingers & invisible legs that fly & smash the final
throne the minuscule lie the throat & fist of the general the boss the
shocked supervisor it is the earth with its moss & its deep ovaries &
sperm that spill their honey & sweat & unleash the rain & purify with
their heat it is the earth that recognizes the squadron of planes the
uniform of shadows & silver the barracks of business & anguish & tanks
of hired blood the flag of iodine dust & rage in the center of camp the
tongue of the American president twisting with nuclear spit

Earth

Send the women of your blood like suns
Send the workers of your branches like lightning
Send the guerrillas of your peaks like tigers

259

Earth

Amid the metropolitan streets
Amid the alleys of fear
Amid the Honduran refugee camps
Amid the Guatemalan slums
Amid the Argentine cells
Amid the Lacandón lakes of Chiapas
Amid the municipalities of El Salvador
Amid the avenues of Chile
Amid the thorns of Jamaica
Amid the storms of Haiti
Amid the phosphorescent jungles of Brazil
Amid the liquid nights of South Africa
Amid fever
Amid death

To make a quake of victory
to make a cluster of liberated world
to make a song in flood

It is the earth
It is the earth
that triumphs.

From *Akrílica*, 1989.

PYRAMID OF SUPPLICATIONS

Just read the headlines:

First Tremor's Toll Reaches
2,000 Confirmed Dead—Sept. 21, 1985

Everytime I walk Mexico City
I smell petroleum, it's so sweet.
I change into someone else.

I am a swanky Chicano boppin' down San Juan de Letrán
Talking about La Colonia del Niño Perdido where
My mother's from or I am rappin' about the next train
To Veracruz or

I am just heading toward La Torre Metropolitana
To make a deal with the literary honchos—

How about a special supplement on New Raza Poetry
From California, the Southwest?
(Who would travel so far to get published?)

I am from here.
A stranger that never left.

The streets are lined with hands,
Small ones, begging.

Now, her hands, his hands are underground;
Still asking, tangled in a crevice, falling, still expecting,
Groping for her father's chair, descending,
Still reaching for the warmth of a cardboard shield,
Tumbling under the final tear of their miniature candle,
He screams for his lover's shawl, his daughter's memory
Slipping further into the arms of this anonymous war.

I can hear the rosaries behind the quivering backs
Still turning over her fingers. Still waiting for his salvation.

Still darkening.

Perhaps, foodstuffs will be distributed to the living.
Who knows?

Undoubtedly,
The presidents will talk about reconstruction
And the tourists will travel without fear (again).

Will we be here still falling?
Who will write about it?

I have never wanted to surrender,
Not even to death's sudden ripening glow.

But, here, in this final burial,

There are no real choices.

The blue baby and the dignitary with a brief mustache,
A young Mexican Adelia studying to be an agronomist,
Chico, the shoeshine kid and the PSUM revolutionary
Are alive still, all alive

In this dark carousel
Of no mercy and no forgiveness.

From *Facegames*, 1987.

Playin' Fiddle on the Steps of
La Galería de la Raza, S.F., 1983

AZTLÁN CHRONICLES, VOL. 7, NO. 2

Yolanda M. López shoots the foto Yolanda who paints her
face on a sketch pad with a charcoal pencil & the face is
the face long Olmec curled & spark eyed her hair pours
down so she looks through the lens & tells me to do some-
thing it must be late October Cecilia Brunazzi is putting
the poster together for the reading of my second book
Exiles of Desire on 11/13/03 at La Galería where we go
smell the paints & ogle the porcupine earrings María
Pinedo sells to be worn by a mysterious lover in white I
bow down with a melody in the harlequin air on Bryant &
24th where Kush sang in 1981—"For the people, for the peo-
ple, for the people . . ."

HOW TO ENROLL IN A CHICANO STUDIES CLASS

Circa 1967-2006

HOW TO ENROLL IN A CHICANO STUDIES CLASS

Spring '68,
struttin' down Westwood.

You don't know how good I felt when I saw a whole grupo of raza at UCLA in '68 from barrios like Wilmas, Norwalk, Whittier, Bakersfield (and Chicano Studies was still a dream). We had rushed the Chancellor, told him he had to share *el pastel,* give us some slack (of course we stormed the administration, a la brava). Puro chocolate, at last—el Cricket combing his hair into the shape of a goose outside the chemistry building. Speaking out: la Adelaida & la Gloria M.— una güera y la otra prieta, una en teatro, la otra pre-law. Never felt so de aquéllas, even when the frats put up a sign pledging students. Sign said: "No Zapatas Allowed." No problem, me & el Edda, Rana, and Monsiváis took care of it. A baby Molotov, at midnight—the East L.A. method. Good thing it didn't go off. But, they got el mensaje. We invented Chicano Studies, con manos limpias en las mañanas, demanding our rights (this sounds old now but we did demand our rights). With our language, our home-poems, our long walks and fasts for justice—Delano, Sacra, Coachella. I can say this. This was our starting point, a healing net across the borders churned with brown clay, rain clouds, open arms, yerbas, a single leaf from the eucalyptus, for each one of us. This is all you need. Breathe in, breathe out, this green wind, makes you strong.

From *Notebooks of a Chile Verde Smuggler,* 2004.

CHICAN@ LITERATURE 100

First of all, you are not going to find this stuff at the mall, in one of those flashy pendejada shops. Maybe you'll have to quiet yourself down, listen to yourself, try pintura for a few days, maybe weeks, take rainy walks, make small mirrors, rake the front yarda, listen to the rake speak, do a mandado for your abuelita if she still lives (do it w/o berrinches), dig up black dirt on the trail in the forest, carry twisted wood and leave it at the edge of the road with good words between you and a squirrel behind the trees, go back and find the seed-voices, the ones that raised you, the letters that arrived with your red-green spirit, the ancient songs way deep inside.

From *Notebooks of a Chile Verde Smuggler*, 2004.

Mission Street Movements

AZTLÁN CHRONICLES, VOL. 3, NO. 12

Had to write it down for the Ph.D. at Stanford just didn't
know how to say how to put it down how to talk it or even
how to think it that's it how to think it you just look
around the streets the apartments the populations popping
out clapping from the cafés the tiny lanes from the diners
the sawed-off alleys the faces made of dingy & ebullient
life floppy in bathrobes bottles clanking spattered in moon-
light & beers & free ideas & stone-cold riffs of brutal
things how to write the poet lives the artists the talkers
the spoken tribe from Valencia Street all the way from César
Chávez to Market the collectives the women groups the gay
cadres the Latinos kickin' outta Harrison Street Chinatown
medicine kids the Blacks on the stoop in the Haight the
breakdancers falling apart at night by the light posts white
boys white girls the hauled piers of green screaming light
in their eyes all the wires electrified with Thai salsa &
the little reading places with their flamenco reddish wedge
tables & candle winos roaring international information &
bagels & horns & ol' chewed up trumpeteers the harmonies &
the consequences of all this & the interiors of the poetry
crates & corner box bananas & Warhols on Chevys & insane
mothers talking about AIDS & quivering fathers in a trance
singing tenor mariachi dueling on the corner before church
time at St. Peter's & the new girlwomen on platforms audi-
tioning for the prize at the 24th Street cultural street
fair in tight-hip silver slink dresses with flags wrapped
around their bellies & the tiny men on stage itching their
pants with their fingers the streets outside staggering
sideways shaking shook

PHOTO-POEM OF THE CHICANO MORATORIUM 1980/L.A.

Circa 1980-1983

Lil' Ray Segura & Lil' Ricky Robles on Whittier Blvd., East L.A., Chicano Moratorium, 1980. PHOTO: GUSTAVO ARIAS

PHOTO–POEM OF THE CHICANO MORATORIUM 1980/ L.A.

PHOTO 1. PILGRIMAGE.

The march is holy. we are bleeding. the paper crosses unfold after ten years. stretching out their arms. nailed. with spray paint. onto the breasts of the faithful. followers. they bleed who we are. we carry the dead body. dragging it on asphalt *America*. we raise our candle arms. our fingers are lit. in celebration. illuminating. the dark dome of sky. over Whittier Boulevard. below. there are no faces. only one. eye. opening its lens. it. counts the merchants locking iron veils. silently secretly. as we approach. their gold is hidden. they have buried diamond sins in the refrigerators. under the blue velvet sofas. they are guarding a vault. of uncut ring fingers. the candles sweat. who tattooed the santo-man on our forehead? Ruben Salazar. we touch the round wound with saliva the clot of smoke. a decade of torn skin. trophies. medallions of skull. spine. and soul. spilled. jammed. on the grass. gone forever. beneath the moon-gray numbers of L.A.P.D. August 29 1970. running. searching for a piece. of open street. *paraíso negro*. pleading to the tear-gas virgins. appearing over the helmet horns of the swat-men. iridescent. we walk. floating digging deep. passing Evergreen cemetery. passing the long bone palms shooting green air. stars. as we count the death stones. burning. white.

rectangles. into our eyes. processions have no gods. we know. they know. the witnesses. on the sidewalks the thirty-two-year-old mother with three. children. no husband. by the fire hydrant. the bakers. the mechanics leaning on the fence. spinning box wrenches. in space. the grandfather on the wheelchair saluting us. as we pass. as we chant. as we scream. as we carry the cross. a park with vendors appears ahead

PHOTO 2. OASIS/WE GATHER/AUDIENCE/WIDE-ANGLE

For El Aztleca de San Diego.

We drink tropical waves.unknown lips of sun & fragrant oils slip. down our backs. *nos reímos camaradas.* we gather & we scope the elements the cop helicopter will never invade our lake it will never drink our perfume. today we make this crazy speck of twin-blades blow. away. with our eyes. la Kathy from East Los. el David & his chavalo Noel. la Eva rapping with César el Bobby. Valentín & Francisco. we slap the air hard. pulsating. opening the rock. around our bodies. liquid. flesh. pouring. circling. entering the grass. el saxofón blows hearts & lightning & Félix sings quarter notes. *¡chale con el draft!* pulling at his chinese beard. El Aztleca talks about the cultural center in San Diego. power plays in the dance group. we pull at the grass snipping stems. making incense for miniature altars. who can fill the chasms in the corners around the shoes? the black net stockings silhouette cliffs & shifting gravel stains the shirttails. a question mark of buttons surrounds the waters. flashing against the flat buildings. we gather. in the light

PHOTO 5. SUNSET

People leave. slowly. taking their cameras. back to Stockton.
Colorado. back. to Fetterly Street some. pick up the cans. the leaflets.
crossed out & filled in with addresses. the vendors close up & pack
into the vans. looking back. the fence remains. bitten with rust. sharp
coils. making a crown out of iron y's and x's over the sun. some of us
go to the bar on the corner. we. leave slowly with a few extra rolls of
negatives. black & white who got the viejito in his wheelchair? or the
Varrios Unidos group with the placas? shouting *what do you want?*
answering (the vato with the hoarse voice) *justice! when do you want it?*
now! the stage spins. out acrylic mural images. la mujer. con un rifle.
together with a man. marching out of the plywood Emmanuel
Montoya painted. jumping high. into the wet grass. doing steps of
being shot. suddenly. opened up. by the torque of bullets. a gas
cartridge pierces the belly of the woman. her imaginary rifle
disappears the policeman lifts his wooden pipe. strikes one. 2. three
4. five. 6. seven. 8. nine. ten. times. on her back. she falls
falls.falls.bleeding.her lips screaming through the tempest *don't leave*

PHOTO 6. NIGHT/AFTERMATH/THE MIME
AT FIGUEROA ST./TRI-X

For Adrian Vargas.

The mime moves. lightly. he teaches us political ballet step. by step.
his eyes have bodies. that stretch. far into the air. of Latin America.
tiller-woman. tiller- man. beneath the *patrón*. the military. *La Junta*
fevers in plantations. deliriums. in haciendas. still El Salvador. light
bodies. explode in cathedrals the yearning chests multiply. into

277

honeycomb spilled muscles. flayed. floating. caught in the bamboo gyrations of his eyes. featherweight tendons. shutter as he snaps the head left. staring into the room of people on chairs. lined up. against the off-white wall stamped with photo 1. the march. photo 2. a woman speaking. photo 3. leaders at the microphone. photo 4. undercover agents. photo 5. people fleeing. cut. dying in 1970. he stares. over the banister. past our shoulders. past. the gallery wall. seeing us. rumble murmur. rumble. scream. pushing. we sweat. smoking jive. with cans of beer. wet offerings. to unknown deities. seeing the moist walls behind us. open the single eye. pointing steady. shooting. across the horizon moon swaying its tattooed flesh through the city. compounds of swollen curtains. an apartment with a hallway altar. a boy passes by the crucifix bronze. body of Christ. guarding a bouquet of plastic day-glo roses. a blue candle vase. tapping light rhythms on the ceiling. whispering lips of smoke at the. end. an opaque window. shut. closing out the night of violent winds and soft movements.

From *Exiles of Desire*, 1983.

278

MISSION STREET MANIFESTO

First read at the Grand Piano Café, Haight Street, S.F., 1981.
For all varrios.

Blow out the jiving smoke the plastic mix the huddling straw of the
dying mind and rise sisters rise brothers and spill the song and sing
the blood that calls the heart the flesh that has the eyes and gnaws
the chains and blow and break through the fuse the military spell the
dreams of foam make the riff jump the jazz ignite the wheel burn the
blade churn rise and rise sisters rise brothers and spill the song and
sing the blood that calls the ancient drums the mineral fists the
rattling bones of gold on fire the lava flow the infinite stream the
razor wave through the helmet the holy gun the Junta the seething
boot shake it do the shing-a-ling the funky dog of sun and moon pull
out the diamonds from your soul the grip of light the stare of stars rip
the wires invade the air and twist the scales and tear the night go
whirling go singing go shining go rumbling go rhyming our
handsome jaws of tender truth our shoulders of sweating keys to
crack the locks the vaults of hands the dome of tabernacle lies and
rise sisters rise brothers and spill the song and sing the blood that
calls out swing out the breathing drums the tumbling flutes the
hungry strings and spin a flash deep into the sorrow of the silent skull
the vanquished lips the conquered song the knot in the belly of earth
break out through the fenders the angel dust kiss the methadone
rooms go chanting libre chanting libre go chanting libre go libre *La*

Mission libre *El Salvador* libre *La Mujer* the will of the worker now the
destiny of children libre blow out the jiving smoke the plastic mix the
huddling straw of the dying mind the patrolling gods the corporate
saints the plutonium clouds strike the right the new Right to crucify
the right to decay the triple K the burning cross the territorial rape
game and stop the neutron man the nuclear dream the assassination
line the alienation master the well-groomed empire the death suit
and rise and rise libre libre and rise and rise and rise libre and rise
sisters rise brothers and spill the song and sing the blood that calls
blow out the jiving smoke the plastik mix the huddling straw of the
dying mind
forever
forever
forever

From *Exiles of Desire*, 1983.

Last Incantation for the Coming of the Sixth Sun, 1974

AZTLÁN CHRONICLES, VOL. 7, NO. 9

For Fernando.

There was dawn in our eyes blowin' modern ancient & soft
juvenile in T-shirts & Dashikis & sharp zoot like suits
baggy subterranean pants & liquid husky freckled breasts
loose shirts & skirts naked see-thru & elegant sexy &
mango-colored skin anxieties & a big band sound in our
heads it all happened in '74 the beginning & the end of it
all the movimiento the chicano thing it all came to a rum-
blin' stop pop alto saxophone swinging nostalgic yeah yeahs
at the Fine Arts Palace near the Marina El Sexto Sol lit-
erature conference where I arrived with Alurista & Fernando
Alegría so I hooked up & rolled in with my guitar from San
Diego wilderness mural & poetry lives read Papaya had just
typed it out at the Centro & I didn't know why the audience
was barking & laughing & wild standing applauding because
the fruit was sexual really sexual in Puerto Rico & the
Rican brothers & sisters in the seats were swinging with
it what can I tell you everyone was there Hernández Cruz
Roberto Vargas Nina Serrano the bards of San Pancho the
crooners from the southlands the hands-down filmmakers from
Berkeley the school without walls people the Native Ameri-
can brother tearing up his electric guitar on stage so I
put on a hat a jazzy auburn love hat from Murguía's rack
near the Excelsior before we drove on ceviche & smokes to
green street downstairs joint César's Latin Club with Mongo
slappin' congas North Beach that was the year when we

jumped the trains in Mexicali & headed south to Mexico City
50 hours straight for the Quinto Festival de Teatros Chi-
canos yeah & joined up with the Mexican & Latinamerican
artists poets & street theatres El Salvador Chile Argentina
Colombia eating tortillas & beans sleeping on nothing
freezing floors & printing out newsletters for the day's
read political we moaned & drank we did the new work at
Cine Negrete Cine Comonfort we bused to Alamos Veracruz to
the tobacco collectives & sang worker songs & ditties about
class & big change said what we had to say with mandolins
& cigars & hot beers when we came back our faces had bro-
ken into our new faces & new limbs of basil & cloud blood
& that wet universe mystery creationpulse plasma thing in
the mouth of the volcano & then guess what we walked away

PAPAYA

Circa 1974

PAPAYA

First read at the Sexto Sol Chicano Latino Literature Conference,
Palace of Fine Arts, S.F. 1974.
For Jorge & Lourdes.

hey
sister & bro'
don't walk so slow
papaya yellow sun on your
shoulder
se cae & spill seeds
papaya
es de allá y de aquellas
quetzalcoatl fruit bro'
sister
simon!
feed on sweet tropical jugo
you know carnala
tu corazón papaya
rotates
& germinates
ciclos
cycles
rivers & ruedas no carruchas!
ruedas!
rings of power
open flow awakenings

don't move your mouth
mueve tu papaya
y watcha carnal
tu cuerpo
tu barrio
tu tierra tu cielo tropical
give a new rhythm
papaya

papaya
papaya
vapaya
payava
paya paya
va
ya va
ya va
paya
pa paya
pa
pa
ya
ya
va
papaya
pa ya

From *Rebozos of Love*, 1974.

ROLLIN' INTO TAOS IN AN AZTEC MUSTANG

For Florencio Guerrero Yescas, RIP, & Esplendor Azteca, 1974,
and Reggie Cantú who hosted us in Taos.

17 miles south of San Diego, in Tijuana next the Hipódromo. Been
here before, betting on hungry dogs with tiny T-shirts racing after a
handkerchief dipped in hot salsa. Talking to the Mexican consulate
man. (Since I got the *jale* at the Centro Cultural in San Diego, I bring
la gente over from México—on an artist visa.) Esplendor Azteca, I tell
the consulate man. Five native dancers from Mexico City, hardwood
tambores, copal incense in ancient burners, two thousand green beads,
yarn, and the taste of petroleum, flavor of licorice from growing up
Mexicano, from stalling between oil refineries, fortune-telling
parakeets, candy makers—and exile.

The troupe: Florencio, *el maestro,* with the cherubic face of Pedro
Infante (he's the one that taught Amalia Hernández at Bellas Artes in
Mexico City) makes the *danzante* costumes with anything that you can
find, a Virgen de Guadalupe etched with needles or with a quarter on
a round slice of metal, a 7-Up can, for example. Piolín, from varrio
Tacubaya, a rib cage shaped like New York, puckers his mouth when
he talks, says he's never going back to La Capital. Conejo, short, dark
with the face of George Harrison, ex-Beatle. When Conejo wants to
leave he says, "*Les gotas,*" when things are difficult, "*La hacemos, las*

hacemos. " Lázaro—he's the one who listens to Florencio's stories about *la danza,* how to care for the fire, how to make friendship with the flame, so it won't burn you—he keeps these stories, in his young silence nourishes them with his own design. Chepe-chepe, short for José and Pepe doesn't look the part. His hair is short, curly—then he's got a goofy laugh, shuffles instead of walking the line, "Me voy a casar en los estados," he says, rubbing his *penacho.* And Cerillo, from Tacubaya too—a tall, thin boy, a matchstick with big wet eyes. He's the drummer, stoic, sad—precise.

When we got to San Diego from Tijuas, I asked Alurista and Irene if Esplendor could stay with us. (I had a room upstairs overlooking a eucalyptus on Grove Street. In the closet one pair of pants, one pair of string huaraches, a couple of *camisas,* a white cotton one, a see-through green Hindu shirt, and a guitar that I borrowed from the Centro Cultural de la Raza housed in an occupied water tank in Balboa Park.

Grove Street is famous. This is where San Diego Raza attempted to build a Marxist Indian commune in early '71; ask Viviana Zermeño, or Alurista's old roommate, Jorge "Krishna" Gonzales.

So, we tied a red flannel strip on our foreheads before we left for the Floricanto II festival in Austin, Texas—our first stop. We figured the red strip would identify us among thousands of poets, dancers, and *artistas.* When we passed El Paso in Mario Aguilar's white Mustang, I thought of my mother, Lucha, who grew up in el Segundo Varrio. I thought of la *calle* Kansas, la Stanton, Paisano Drive, la Overland, la Segunda, la Tercera, la Poplar—the streets were fragments of an incomplete story I carried. Part of me still lived there, an unknown infant in half-shapes, wondering for the other lost half.

I wanted to stop, walk into myself again, but we didn't have time.
Conejo (who didn't know how to drive) popped a *llanta* thirty meters
from Sonora, Texas, a small town with one gas station and two fast
curves. The Mustang was the kitchen: while Mario drove, Piolín cut
green tuna cans and made cracker tacos. On the road, cracker tacos
are smart. Smarter than eggplant or spaghetti. We passed Johnson
City and talked about LBJ as gateposts and nettles washed by the
fenders. Viet Nam was still in the air. The only thing that saved me
from the draft was a bad case of hepatitis, otherwise I would have
gone on the road, like Patadas, a carnal, still hiding out in Santa
Monica—Colby Street, in a garage with tree-stump end tables, a
Bartlett pear tree—this was back in 1969.

Lázaro asked me about Floricanto. I told him, "These are our songs,
this is how our gente comes together—our poetry, carnal." First
Floricanto was in '73, November 13 and 14, just a year ago, at USC.
That's where I met raúlrsalinas—the small r is for Roy. Most of the
time he keeps this a secret. He was just out of Leavenworth. Red
bandanna, Levi's *planchados*, spit-shined *calcos*, and a black belt, as
thin as a toothpick. Miguel Méndez and Tomás Rivera read from
their new *libros*, *Peregrinos de Aztlán* and . . . *y no se lo tragó la tierra*. They
looked serious, even though they still combed their *greña* like
pachucos, especially Miguel. They wore formal light-colored short
sleeves too, but I recognized the language, the tone, what they were
saying. Teresa Palomo Acosta talked about el Teatro de los Niños
from Pasadena. She was writing plays, poetry plays; this hadn't been
done before. Veronica Cunningham was coming out with her sexual
politics, ahead of all of us. She read

when all the yous
of my poetry
were really
she or her
and
i could never…

Veronica paused,

no
i would never
write them
because
of some fears
i never even wanted
to see.

Zeta Acosta, the Brown Buffalo, East Los, Raza Lawyer and San
Francisco nomad (originally from the San Joaquín Valley) stood up,
asked the techs to turn the theater lights off. Then he read chapter 8
from his new novel—*The Revolt of the Cockroach People*. About a
Chicano, named Robert Fernández, "suicided" by the L.A.P.D., a
Chicano on a metal autopsy table with nothing left, not even face
skin. Zeta lost the battle with Noguchi, the coroner at the time in Los
Angeles—the body decomposed, case closed. Lack of evidence on the
Pacific edge of America. That was the last time I saw Zeta, his body
blocked out in black. Only voice, full of breath, almost as if he was
praying; I noticed it when he read the last page and asked Robert for
forgiveness.

Forgive me Robert,
for the sake of the living brown,

Zeta said, as if he was dying too. Shortly after the festival Zeta disappeared in Mexico; off the coast of Michoacán, they say, no one knows.

Austin was full of sky. Instead of pyramids, there were clouds, tints of green, sandstone, slate blue. At UT Austin, we danced, I barely knew the danzas, *la del Sol,* for example. I forgot the names of the others. There was one where we squat, keep the feet steady then go into swift circles above the ground, flesh spins, into lost centuries. My legs whiter than *arroz con leche.* Mario had the same problem. If I could do it, he could do it. If he did it, I did it. Florencio didn't mind. He liked the way we talked our Azteca history; Indian books, Egyptian maps salvaged from the San Diego Public Library on "E" Street. After the reading and performances like the one Cecilio García-Camarillo did using a tiny radio and kung fu moves, after Américo Paredes read on Sandino, way after Reyes Cárdenas, the only Chicano poet with *canas* at the time, we ran into Tomás Atencio, a *cuentista* from Peñasco, New Mexico.

Why don't you come up to our pueblo and dance? Seven-thirty, in the town hall, he said. *Orale.* Two days later, we filled the Mustang with more tuna cracker tacos. The wind blew our drums and luggage off the roof on the way into Santa Fe. Stuff was hanging off the side for about twenty-five miles, wind whipping the way forward. Two hours late but gente were still waiting, huddled sombreros and long dresses. So, Mario and me strapped on our *guitarras* and sang "El Picket Line"

291

and some songs we had written together with Alurista. Songs like
"Vamos caminando hacia la vida real," "Nubes de lucha" and
"Altísimo corazón." We were Okier than Hank Williams, more
organic than Maharishi Mahesh. Florencio and the Aztec boys were
in the back of the wooden stage changing their *ropa*. I could hear
Piolín cuss, said he couldn't fit into his bikini pants from all the *refín*
in Austin. Refín was the gift of the danzante, to celebrate after small
sacrifices, fasts, the giving of oneself to the gods and goddesses
through one's body made of roads, clouds—all in motion.

After the show, we ate sopaipillas, frijoles colorados con salsa and *chicos
con carne de res*. We had never seen that kind of food. Sopaipillas like
erotic *quesadillas* blown up and dipped in red chile sauce from
Chimayó. (If you box your *orejas* right, they'll turn to sopaipillas.) The
viejitas from Chimayó grow the *chiles colorados*, in front of their painted
adobe houses, they dry them; *nietos* and *nietas* harvest them. *Chicos*,
baby corn kernels, pearled yellow thorns that centuries ago turned into
sweet milk drops, translucent, to cook in the frijoles with fresh ground
beef. After this I wanted to stay in Peñasco. But we kept on when Tomás
said, "You should look up Reggie Cantú, in Taos; he's part of La
Academia, you know. He's up there with el Arnie Trujillo. *Están bien
locos.*" La Academia was like the Centro Cultural in San Diego. A place
in Peñasco where the local artistas got their jales done, in their own
style, the *comunidad* walks in, eats *cena* on the table, sings—even el
Loquito de Peñasco pushes his eyes up. Tomás told us about el Reggie
and el Arnold. One was a poet and playwright, *el otro* a photographer.
"Maybe they can get you some jales in the schools while you're there,"
Tomás told us at the cena. "Les gotas," Conejo said.

Drive into Taos. The first thing you notice is that Taos is surrounded by a ring of blue-colored mountains; their journey ended there, after one long darkness when the universe became light. Their bluish mist speaks of this. They are sacred, I remembered Tomás saying that. That's where the Taos Indians take the young boys so that they can become men, with chants, admonishments, the giving of pain inside the body, their new eyes, sleepless moss at dawn. They stay up there fasting, praying, finding their life. We called Reggie from a gas stop on a hill before we rolled into town.

The light was sharp on the stones. Sagebrush, sky—a lizard on a sparkling dark rock, blowing in, blowing out. We followed the trail for a while, taking in the flavor of the red earth, the invisible oil of the plants, we looked down at Taos, open country, Indian pueblos, reddish, brown, soft, a favored cup of the wind gods.

Reggie was a thin guy with funny quickness something like a Chicano Woody Allen, a clean one. He took us to Anita Rodríguez's *cantón*, a circular eight-room adobe house. Anita was an *enjarradora,* one who smoothes adobe clay on the inside, follows its shape, into a hearth, a fireplace. The inner sheath of her *casa*—a sand blanket folded over the shape of the adobe into a brownish bowl of sparkles, the fire hole, where the fire shows itself blue, red, blue, an earth-stone womb made with her hands. We stayed a few days, ate good *tortillas de harina,* carried *leña*, made fire in the morning, fed *la estufa*—this house kept us warm, outside the blue-powdered cape was infinite snow.

We met Arnie, *el cuadrado* with thick glasses. He seemed to know the same stories that Reggie knew, about the pueblo *curandero, el viejito,* Don Jaramillo, for example.

Reggie and Arnie made a few *visitas* and got us invited to perform at Taos Junior High. On the bleachers, the children were clay brown, with clear eyes, black torches of hair. I had never seen Indios and Chicanos at the same time, sitting in the same row looking like each other, not even in the heights of Ramona Mountain, east of San Diego. This city of blue songs taught me this was possible. And their kindled voices: I could hear all their voices with every step I took in the dance circle. This was good.

Something moved inside me, a little above my stomach pulling me forward, blowing sweetness into my lungs, up to my forehead. The flavor was in my mouth too. The next day we danced at Taos Indian School, then inside Taos Pueblo Church. Wasn't sure about the church, it was a sacred place for the Taos Pueblo people. Who was I? What dance could I offer? What was I carrying forward? Did I have mysteries, ancestors? I had forgotten about shelter, about seeking, all this, about dreaming the way one asks questions, to a sudden sparrow knocking. Wasn't used to offering a dance or even visiting. Wasn't used to anything like this. But I danced out of the lightness that I carried inside.

Florencio said a few words to the elders, very few, maybe he just smiled, gazed into their eyes and they gazed back, bowed their heads a little, in the dark, like birds. Walked in, Florencio, barefoot, his headdress and feathers, holding up the *incensario* lit with sharp flecks of *copal*. We followed the sweet smoke: Piolín, Lázaro, Conejo, Cerillo, Mario and me. Stepped through the blue roots, the spirals of tree smoke copal up the Taos altar; there was reddish corn, star shapes in husk-leaf, yellowish flesh, seeds in gourds, enameled saucers, other figures, full of light, didn't look directly at them. Was dancing. That's all, a long way from home, Austin in my blood, Peñasco, Velarde, Pojoaque, Española, the trails that led me to this humble prayer house my home wasn't here or there, just drifting, nowhere, homeless, I could feel it moving my legs, my belly tight through the circle, we were weaving our shoulders through the wet darkness of the brown church in step with the carved drum inside greater circles, blue mountains, blessing circles above blue mountains.

From *Night Train to Tuxlta*, 1994. Revised.

The Third Aztlán

AZTLÁN CHRONICLES, VOL. 5, NO. 13

The first Aztlán is in the books the ones we stole from
Royce UCLA library in '67 & stuffed into our shirts down
our pants to the banana bush pad in Santa Monica where we
laid out the section of the Liberated Knowledge F1219 to
F1235 everything a Chican@ needs to know to become a full-
fledged mutant of lower learning mad & stumbling on
Saturday night unbelievable crazy ecstasy all about the
archaeological layers of tombs & mounds & village forma-
tions of the first social groups in the bellybutton of the
Américas valley of México multi-conditioned for ecologi-
cal diversity & population flora & fauna groove & Che
Guevara's diaries & Fidel's legal defense against the
Batista regime & the black bold wide face of Olmec grand-
fathers bowing down the tropical floors the second Aztlán
is the chicano Aztlán that blown-out colonized land grab
1848 Treaty of Guadalupe Hidalgo still waiting in the
waiting room the Aztlán Alurista reconjured in a San Diego
barrio rented room with anthro books on his desks & bossa
nova playin & thelonious monk albums & a red beret & more
ceviche on the table & out yellow wax peppers this Aztlán
the one everyone talks about the second Aztlán singing
songs from tijuana to utah in cave glyph arias the one
Cecilio Orozco proved in the books well yeah the third
Aztlán you can call Wirikuta the Original Place the Place
of the First People Huichol Nayarita Jalisco Zacatecas
triangle the Wixarika ambassadors nomads to el norte in
'70 I met the poet singer healer cantor mara'akame Ramón
Medina Silva knower & speaker of the third Aztlán the
original Aztlán the one we were searching for when I

ambled to his concrete blown-out shanty by the highway to
Guadalajara next to a Fanta soda stand gas station he said
he knew I was coming in from L.A. I asked how how how he
said Tauyepá told me Tauyepá then he pointed up past the
diesel smoke to the sun

HACE MUCHOS AÑOS HUICHOL

Circa 1969-1971

Ramón Medina Silva, mara'akame, at healing ceremony, El Colorín Rancho.
Nayarit, Huichol Nation, Mexico, 1970.

(HACE MUCHOS AÑOS HUICHOL)

First read at the Yolteotl Chicano Arts Expo, UCLA, March 1973.

hace muchos años huichol
montañas ground maizitos red
plumas wrapped en bronce aquí
yo nací
para siembras y cantar
ruturi flor de la lira tuyamía
tamboras venado cuero
jorongo de la tierra diosa
siembra
para deep cantos cantas una
toda vida oval tauyepá sol
cara
tuyamía
enteros mil cuerpos
desnudos semilla fires
suben
de las sombras dark spiral sangre
secos
dry frias matas mares
las conchas campanas glow mi padre
tauyepá águilas sol
¿lo miras?

dark huipiles
lanos lana mugre carne
en el llano serpiente cara wrapped
odios
hechos a mano partida corazón
chupan la carne frías entrañas sabores
maizita ciega
cascaros hambras umbar alambres
he hambres en cielo sin sol
angustias tilichis mi
cuerpo miles of trenzas rotas
siento las llamas latifundios
no brillan la vida
corazones huicholes
dragging feathers wilted
en mis guitarra milpas
el chapulino se fué
no quiero
el mundo millas en carbón semillas murallas
dark estrellas
verdes
caras
sin ojos frutas hojas bloom mira
¡mira!
eres águila be born la luz
bendita rainbow
estambres caldos ground corn
jorongos jacaranas
trees pueblito frutas rico
canta huichol

zarape tejida fértil rebozos
frutas redondas sol ancho
amor tuyamía
flowing
foreheads venas vengan woven sierras llenas
mariposas
tejuinos en la nochis quemando
ocote
rezas sudo
ocote humos mares
hirviendo espejos kingdom alas en tus trenzas
tuyomío
reino ground star corn of
quetzales creciendo un pueblo
cantas tambores venado
spill chorros las sangres podrida
en el vientre del campos
selfmilpas no crecen
sacrificates el corazón & walk the sky jugos
radiant ground corn ombligo
abierta breathing dios rayos weaving
sol
amor
wisdom sudor
violeta red ground corn
entero pueblo to sprout

El Colorín, Huichol rancho, after corn harvest ceremony, Sierra Nayar, Nayarit, Huichol Nation, Mexico, 1970.

(CORAZÓN, SIN DIVISIÓN)

corazón sin división
llama roja
sin humo
corazón sin división
rebozo verde
lana de dios
llano de magueyes
corazón sin división
mujer de estrellas mojadas en el mar
sin tu espejo
corazón sin división
yo no puedo ya mirar
me dicen que'l tiempo importa
corazón sin división
pero tu sangre es de siete soles
y tu beso
los rayos rosas del amanecer
corazón sin división
en la playa de pescadores
y en las minas de carbón
corazón sin división
haciendo *muvieris*
varas de energía
en las manos del Huichol
pa' curar los hechiza'os

corazón sin división
venado azul
flor de la montaña
maíz del sudor
corazón sin división
espacio negro
espacio blanco
halcón de luz
mariposa de obsidiana
corazón sin división
materia espiral
energía sin fin
corazón sin división
mar de Quetzalcoatl
sangre de Cristo
huella de Buddha
tinta del relámpago justiciero
corazón sin división
alabanza sin palabras
pintura sin paredes
espiga de carne viva
vestida de manta
Levi's khakis calcos
y flores de algodón
que nacen
en el fil pizca'o
corazón sin división
corazón de corazones
corazón sin división
tu hermosura no es palabra

y tu presencia no es
mentira

From *Rebozos of Love,* 1974.

Guadalupe de la Cruz Ríos, Huichol shaman. Occupied adobe by the road to Guadalajara. Tepic, Nayarit, 1970.

Soulsacrifice(s)

AZTLÁN CHRONICLES, VOL. 1, NO. 10

The Santa Monica pad in '69 was a cauldron a fury nonstop
joint of draft-dodger acid meditators failed molotov dream-
ers pintos going back to school with needles stuck in their
arms Puerto Rican serious dudes in white pants & lovers
knocking the door down the FBI looking for Baby Patadas in
the back hiding & fancy campesino kids come to the big UCLA
from a welfare check to an EOP check all the dwarfed energy
in the universe channeled & raced through those red purple
splashed paint walls busted rivery arteries blessed by Cha-
gall & Rothko & Pollock the stove speckled with instant egg
powder for healthy pizzas & cabinets stocked with papaya
tea & white port & outside next to the peach tree the lam-
inated dull cucumber colored garage where I lived hoochie
coochie listening to Van Morrison & Zappa & Los Panchos &
Coltrane's Prestige album Settin' the Pace & Santana's
Black Magic Woman yeah this is the cavern where we hatched
our plans the university strikes the walkouts the East L.A.
rallies the storms into the administration Murphy Hall
offices the trek to the original third Aztlán the Chicano
Moratoriums the César Chávez trails & Teatro patroncito
Viet Nam skits & new scribble poems & cut your own hair in
the mirror yes & kisses & insomniac tender voices human
lips spilling tearing blowin' going up in fast flames &
gooey electric Les Paul guitar funeral shadows

LISTENING TO SANTANA

Circa 1968-1972

LISTENING TO SANTANA (remix)

For Al Robles,
a charter member of the house, RIP.
For Kathy Ledesma and Rita Ledesma, still going strong.

When one of us dies you can tell.

A swarm of children in black. Notice how El Greco paints us into the barrio scene. The men are short, then elongated, going up into the turbulent skies, stilled by a crazy figure inside and outside: a charcoal Madonna with the face of Martha Graham, except more oval and with a seductive mouth. Their bent, tiny heads glimmer. For a second or two. A couple of shots are heard. Four shots—a military salute for the wrap in the casket—the way my uncle Geno went down into the ground in '57.

Behind tombstones.

Hide and go seek with Chente, my cousin. Both of us have bucktecth and we laugh like girls. Mama is the only one crying, she leans down into the soft earth and pulls up the bluish pit in her soul. When I cry—silence. Sometimes it comes in little beeps. Gets jammed somewhere on my upper back, near the neck. Useless, most of the time. A few years ago I made peace with another uncle, Roberto Q.

Five car nations. We never talked. Made candy, pink-striped bars wrapped in cellophane in his basement. Got busy, later—a poet with four kids. Riding around Stanford in a '54 yellow Ford pickup. Wore bell-bottoms and aced the classes. Except Collier's statistics; you can always catch a Chicano flunking statistics. This was my first folly at Stanford. The second was disappearing for an entire summer in Mexico to live the life of Cagney in Cuernavaca and Brando in Acapulco. At five a.m., hang out the window of the Hotel Regency Presidente—eight floors up. Gaze over the bay, baby, inhale the green air, love the sweetness from the sky. Alcohol from my ledge and gasoline from speedboats and the helicopters, the ones that take you up in a nylon kite for four hundred pesos. Come down and drink gin gimlets in the pools. Make love to a secretary from Tegucigalpa. An accident. That's what I said when I got back.

When my mother died my shirt tightened. Cried for six years. Shaved my mustache. Shaved my head. Wanted to cut myself down to size. Strip the skin off. Because I couldn't feel it. Think of ukuleles, I told myself. Oblong brown chocolate ones with good strings. Or Hawaiian shirts at the National Dollar store in San Diego where we used to go shopping in the fifties; Jergens, Three Roses pomade, khakis for fifth grade. Airplane glue in a sock hanging out with Raymond and Arnold and Miguel. Every ghost boy I know. They show up with my uncles now—smoke rings on my bruised face.

The therapist says, Just a couple of visits. I show my teeth. Is it a peppermint flavor inside my lips? Or is it fire?

Sport a flattop now. Think of the days—original flattop days and Roman Meal bread, soft speckled stuff the doctors prescribed for my mother. My father was alive then too. Makes me laugh when he does his special imitation of a gun going off. Does this the same way he makes dove sounds. Pulls his lower lip down with his thumb and forefinger. Then he breathes backwards.

Cook at least three things, learn, he said.

Rice, the long red pointed kind stewed with burnt tomatoes. Enchiladas, the apartment kind, folded with onions and Kraft cheese. They can be served anywhere to anyone. Char the salsa too, on an iron grill. Mash the green-black pulp inside a stone bowl. The one that rocks on three legs.

◎　◎　◎

I could never figure it out.

What was it? This funny cilantro-shaped fender popping out my chest. Feels like when you swallow a hard-ribbed tortilla chip and it jams in your throat. So you flex your throat muscles. Push it down like a boa, because you are starved. You slide the flared brown tin, way down, but instead of smoothing, the pain sharpens, the chip inflates, jams up again, around the thoracic area, creates its own habitat, lives there a bit, turns into a reddish chrome plate piece.

Then, you are in the Mexican Badlands—the Chicano-Faustian shit hole, the Kafkian one-room apartment where there is a Catholic bag of crazy apple skulls ready to come flying at your cockroach-armored back skin. What do I call myself here?

Wittgenstein couldn't even figure out what he was feeling when he tightened his fingers and folded his palm into a fist. Was it temperature? he asked. Position? Centrality? Or was it clarity? Was it Mayan? Was it Eastern clouds with serpentine illumination? What?

In the autumn of '67, the best I could do was jaunt to Beverly Hills whenever possible, run into Saks Fifth Avenue, treat myself to an Italian long-sleeved shirt. No one expects this. None of my revolutionary friends would ever imagine me going up to the second floor, perishing in the men's section. This has always been my weak side, I admit it. Fine Italian shirts with viridian coloration. French sweaters with an oval neck design—thick weaves in ultramarine. For pants: cherry red extra-thick corduroy and on occasion, pinstripe cinnamon brown, stove pipes—I got this from the Rolling Stones, Brian Jones always wore them.

One time I switched my style and wore a see-through purple shirt that my *novia,* Carol, made from women's maternity fabric. My pants were purple too.

Was in a groove in the autumn of '67.

The only thing that caught me by surprise was Carlos Cinco, a Movimiento buddy stabbed in Venice beach—got in a bad brawl with some beach dopers. Cut bad grass with too much sugar. Came back to our pad, five minutes from the piers, pushing into his distorted stomach, tucking his *tripas* back in.

Late night steak *sanwishes* washed down with sangría. A favorite treat at La Casa Naka, our Chicano pad in Venice. The sangría Hector

Carrillo made was best, especially if he was in one of his furious redemption moods. Hector had a holy streak. He either was stoned on Hieronymus Bosch or Jesus Christ. But, you could always count on Hector to give you the right red feeling for the rest of the day. Hector missed his father. Always talked about him, cried sometimes, said he never met him; his mother had raised him alone in the City of Commerce, an industrial plutonium pit in the middle of Los Angeles. Hector carried a tiny silver chain around his neck, with a locket, where he kept a miniature photo of his dad. I don't think he ever saw or heard from him in all of his seventeen years. It drove Hector to a higher level, I think. We would go up to his pad on Wilshire, smoke up and follow Bosch into the *mole*-draped woods, creep into the shattered eggshell beings that lived there, broken and one eyed. When he made sangría in our kitchen, slamming cut oranges and grapes into a wine-filled tin bucket he'd let his mouth hang open, he would hunch up, mumble words out, like

> *pura piña,*
> *tevoyacurar,*
> *somos Mazatecas*
> *—la liberación is in your mouth, carnal.*

Eyes stretched back.

Carlos got stabbed the same night when I had wolfed an extra-large bag of raw walnuts. Ate so many nuts I had to walk five miles to ease the stone-pain in my rib cage area. Ambled all the way to Malibu. On the way back, I found out about Carlos and then about another *carnal*, a Jewish vato named Stein. Stein's favorite saying was "If you are not on the bus, you're off the bus." His face was washed white, his eyes in a spin. Told me there was a guy OD'd in his tub. Said he tried the cold water thing but it didn't work on the bluish body. He knew this guy, Stein said, he was a member of the Life Force student collective in Santa Monica. I had visited Life Force a few times after I had broken up with my wife who was also Jewish. She had moved out of Venice and joined them for a semester. They were into doorless bathrooms, swiveling bedmates, carrot juice, tahini-banana sanwishes, refrigerator billboards detailing chores and holding intense critique sessions on God, jealousy, fear of the body, and political action. Usually they held these raps in yoga-lotus-sitting postures under large canopies of webbed batik sheets in the living room, candles and fava beans in small plates on the carpeted floors.

I recognized the temperature, the positions of the internal helix, the clarity of ocean alphabets, the distance, and the proximity of the cloud people.

I was a Mexican the same way Bosch was Mexican. I was Mexican or Chicano the same way Wittgenstein was Mexican or Chicano. It was all in his gesture, his search for the feeling when he pressed his skin against his skin. What was it he asked, what was it?

I had left home many years ago. Was living now in a wild-city rampage with a cool bass riff underneath. All I had left were the fast colors, flaring, and scarin', flying. On my Kawasaki, in my '59 flared Mercury without side windows and an oval steering wheel melted down from going too deep into Arizona, on a love-chase, after Margarita del Toboso who was holed up in a village a few miles from Prescott, a tiny thirteen-family town on the opposite slope of the Tonto Forest. I found her two decades later, but she was in San José.

All I had were just a few numbers to play with, a few oblong packs of edgy phrases, and a burning portion of a tiny bridge, the one I reached when I jump-started the Kawasaki. An American bridge. I think all of us wanted to get across this busted bridge-line. Behind us, America, in front of us America. Maybe, the greater questions had to do with the bridge itself. What was it made of? How many could it hold. Why was it burning so fast—

red, yellow, red, red.

From *Night Train to Tuxtla*, 1994. Revised.

From the Skylight Room @ the El Cortez Hotel

AZTLÁN CHRONICLES, VOL. II, NO. 27

When I returned to San Diego in '72 & joined the Centro
Cultural de la Raza something happened some new crazy
thing took place in the mist somewhere between the El
Cortez Skylight Room on the top floor of the ol' El Cortez
hotel where in '66 I had sung French madrigals for Mr. Ezra
Harrison Maxwell's San Diego High group overlooking the
bay & Coronado Island & Tijuana colonias it happened yeah
whooping it up in that sad ochre yellow foggy rocking
water tank almost on Park Avenue facing the Navy Hospital
it happened suddenly you reappeared in new form the new
songs were part of it they made it possible songs sung by
Ricardo Mendoza & Trío Moreno all about Aztlán & the
chords were smooth & dreamy that rich Las Vegas harmony
glittery & spangled in muscat & patchouli & the murals
inside that candlelit dome art centro were part of it the
ones by Guillermo Aranda layered in 3-D jaguar bones &
fangs & deers & military marching machines & the teen
sweat lodge girls that polished turquoise angry nuggets &
the long-hair women that danced stoic round dances & went
to Hopi Land & the hard dudes from National City starting
their lives over carving aztec symbols on fresh chocolate-
brown leather whips & the teatros stretching rags out like
Teatro Mestizo doing Macho Bag & that was the feeling the
fur of a dusty tarantula unveiled & shampooed Victor Ochoa
sketched the architectural plan for the sacred city of
artists something like the Amerindia continental self
Alurista conjured after he found Aztlán in English I had

never seen it or drawn it I was just gasping from all
directions with tawny amulets my mother had given me with
memory-pictures from the old México & the staggering load
& auras of the invented bronze riot lives of Los Angeles
from El Monte to Venice Rose Street congas & organic car-
rot juice batik pantaloons where Moctezuma Esparza &
Esperanza Vasquez lived in a hep dark flat on the main drag
& the S.F. Tropicaleros visiting on occasion with their
midnight smokes & puffed jackets gaunt austere handsome
faces Agustín Lara-like & Katy Jurado-like blowin' poems
while lifting their pants & dresses so yeah even though it
would only last until '74 or so there it was crystal god-
dess & dabbed in pastels yeah there made of one part poetry
flesh one part ancient bones of the lost Américas & one
part luminous blessed blessed blessed magic fire tips with
infinite Mayan eyes at the center

IN THE SACRED CITY OF FLORICANTO

Circa 1970-1974

Miguel with guitar. Zinacantán, Chiapas, 1970.

(AMERINDIA ONE HEART)

This series was first read at Floricanto #1. USC, November 13–14, 1973.

Amerindia
one heart
una tierra
roja burning rain
jewel rising
winging song
weaving light
pueblos
chanting
Amerindia
blazing acre soles
rebozoles
laborando
quetzal maíz
goza rise
cuerpo desnudo
sudando
roja chakira blaze
beads
blossom spiral heart
vidacoatl
pueblos sin fronteras

tierra sin cadenas
caras sin correas
parching milpas fall
the earth will churn
and rise the red dawn of blazing
heart
of raza one
Amerindia
celestial earthen song
rings
our blood pulsando
one purpose
one path
sembrando
reap the sol
ahorasol
Kupurisol
Amerindiasol
frondoso corazol
raíz ardiente
to
one heart rise
rasa rise
la primavera to flow
and churn our destiny
cultivando
laborando
one heart nation
liberando
one heart cosmos

to never fall
to always rise
in our heart
in our land
in our struggle
Amerindia
Amerindia

From *Rebozos of Love*, 1974.

(VÁMONOS A LA KIVA CASA LIBRE)

vámonos a la kiva casa libre
taza llena with our blood with our love
jarro claro
templo to meet and regalarnos la luz
en la kiva
casa de pechos abiertos wide
we must die
to ayer soles de hueso yesterday cuerpos
of hungers to pain thirst to sorrow waterfalls
con el caldo of wisdom in radiant gourds
jícaras corazones de sangre
vámonos a pintar murales en el cielo to sing from our wombs
nourishing mundos nuevos so prophesied
vámonos
to sew with looms and chakira beads
wilted broken pueblos flores to jardines
y paraíso aquí
a guisar to fry to season the fires
glowing new mañanitas today
to dawn
a nacernos
to feel to know and drink el cuerpo nuestro
hermoso to sculpt y sudar mundos
kiva
rebozo redondo lucero del pueblo

From *Rebozos of Love*, 1974.

(DAWNING LUZ)

dawning luz
rosaluz
razaluz
brilla
our path
we
blaze
our
heart
we
speak
lluvia
roja
fuente
song
of
struggle
song
of tierra
song
of sangres
song
of
fuego
raza
ahora

raza
llama
sean
los
pueblos
pueblos
flores
pueblos
libres
la
canción
la
semilla
el
corazón
de
la
nación
Amerindia
Amerindia
Amerindia
sea
incandente
sea
consciente
living
sangres
living
tierra
living

árbol
Amerindia
tree
of
heart
open
flower
divinacoatl
vereda
verdadera
flaming
eagles
voladores
tejedores
weaving
rings
cycles
spiral
space
spiral
time
of
our
heart
to
churn
burning
being
nuevo
ciclo

nuevo
espacio
nuevo
tiempo
consciente
dando
fruto

From *Rebozos of Love*, 1974.

(ARCO IRIS MIL)

arco iris mil
colores whirling come
shining come pouring
a celebrar la tierra tierra nueva to churn to make
una canción to grow to young soil
in our woven hands violetas yellow green lluvia
arco iris
luminosa trenza flores in the sky

> cabeza redonda
> de hijos sonrientes
> embrando la nación vida fresca

yes
in our heart es la luz
we bring del sol ancient father on our head
one thousand pétalos rising flower de maíz

> dulce
> trenza luminosa come

weaving
darkness cuerpos sin lucha luz to vida
a sprouting heart
a sostener
a refrescar cada día a
nutrir
> amor luminoso flaming arco
> iris

From *Rebozos of Love*, 1974.

333

(RENACIMIENTO REVIVAL)

renacimiento revival
de nuestra sangre en nuestras venas
milpas rojas to the sun
casa de águilas volando
claros
espejos de carne brillante of fields
where we toil to reap our hijos semillas
de nuestra cara
constellations of cantos to maíz tierno
renacimiento to mariposa
wings de fuerza to create
to build pillars de hermosura en los caminos
to invent aquí around
our ancient feet pezuñas and hands
that fly con las chuparrosas
to make calor jugo cantar all withering
trees

vamos a respirar otra vez con frutos
a nuestra tierra madre que tiene la
lengua rota muda sin el sabor
de infinitas flores azules and
violeta profunda eterna justicia
to siembras a crecer a sudar jardines
lluvia de nuestra frente montaña
of wisdom

334

que sea
que sí
que siiiiiguen
rosas rosas
mariposas in
amar
sea of sky de luz
brillosas burning olas of
danos give us you
sale y dámenos tenemos hambre
ábrenos y pártenos tu pan
dulcezón
corazón
ricozón
walking
walking
everyou
everwe
everflowing
r
í
o

From *Rebozos of Love*, 1974.

renacimiento rebirth to cosechas always
naciendo en las raíces sacred roots de
vida latiendo trompetas y marimbas
en nuestro corazón

From *Rebozos of Love*, 1974.

(FLOW RIVER RÍO IN EARTHEN SKY)

*Written while Roberto Miranda riffed on his string bass
& Gabriel Stern blew sax at Janns Steps, UCLA, 1971.*

flow river rió in earthen sky
tu
casa
que
siempre crece
síguele y siémbrate
nourishing coming here río atoludo
home
sol blowing alma howl y vaso de risa
siglos of you gleaming sí
lagunas ríos sunbeso you yes
sí tú
ábrete
mírate
rebozo
regozo
rejoys
ríos
guitarrón drops of abrazos pasos
to
here
caras of us
ríos

(WARRIOR WOVEN DAY BREAK STAR ERES)

warrior

woven

day

break

star/ eres

la voz

the

face

of jardín/ yes

swing your shields of toiling heart rhymes & sweet sweat de amor

naked

face

sol/be born

From *Rebozos of Love*, 1974.

(DADOR DE LA VIDA)

Ceremonia para el matrimonio de
Ramón Chunky Sanchez e Isabel Enrique.
Centro Cultural de la Raza, Toltecas en Aztlán,
San Diego, California, 1974.
Liberado tanque de agua, Parque Balboa.

Ceremony for the marriage of
Ramón Chunky Sanchez and Isabel Enrique.
Centro Cultural de la Raza, Toltecas en Aztlán,
San Diego, California, 1974.
Occupied water tank, Balboa Park.

Dador de la vida de tu interior brota el árbol resplendiente
El árbol de la harmonía-energía
El árbol de la luz y la conciencia divina

Señor-señora de la unidad sin fin
Señor-señora de la hermosura terrenal
Señor-señora de la estrella ascendiente
En el corazón de todos los seres

En este día y sitio venimos para hacer nuestra ofrenda
En este día y sitio venimos para abrir nuestro corazón
En este día y sitio venimos para formar nuestra unión

Para merecernos en la gloria de tu amor
Para merecernos en el espíritu de tu paz
Para merecernos en la fuente de tu fuerza
Para merecernos en la labor de tu creación

339

Que el anillo de nuestra vida sea la semilla
De tu dulzura y la flor
De tu calor por el campo de tu vivir

Con este anillo siembro el anillo sin división
El fruto luminoso de nuestro amor
El fruto y fortaleza de nuestra casa
El fruto de nuestra conciencia y acción
El fruto reflejo y espejo de la creadora y el creador

En el viento y la lluvia
En el fuego y la tierra
En la orden que tu has creado nada permanece
Todo lo que se endereza ha de caer
Como la mariposa sus alas abre en el día
La rosa sus brazos dobla en la noche de su vida

En el viento y en la lluvia
En el fuego y en la tierra
En la orden que tu has creado nada permanece
Menos tu consciencia
Menos tu fuerza
Menos la infinidad de tu amor-energía

Enséñanos padre-madre
Creador-creadora de la vida
Y ábrenos el corazón hacia la unión verdadera y absoluta
Por el camino del sacrificio
Por el camino de la disciplina sin violencia
Por el camino de la paz
Por el camino de la medida y el balance

Por el camino de la labor sin ambición
Por el camino del servicio colectivo
Por el camino de la sinceridad tranquila
Por el camino de la claridad sin temor
Por el camino del amor constante
Abrenos el corazón hacia la unión verdadera absoluta

En tu gracias y bendición
Nuestra unión será como el arroyo tranquilo
Que camina sobre las piedras
Como camina las veredas lisas
Que lo beben los seres de la tierra
Y que alcanza el alba y el seno del mar sin fronteras

Señor-señora de la creación
Aquí en este momento y en este sitio
Te ofrecemos el arroyo de nuestra unión

Toma el jugo de mi arroyo para que en tu mar
Yo encuentre mi vida
In lak'ech
Tú eres mi otro yo

Padre-madre de toda creación
Hemos venido a merecernos en tu santa unión

En tu gracia y bendición energía
Elevamos nuestros cantos
Elevamos nuestros rostros
Elevamos nuestros corazones
Asi como el gran árbol eleva su dulce verdad y fruto
En la primavera sin fin

Paz entre todos seres
Amor entre todos seres
Unión entre todos seres

Así sea

From *Rebozos of Love,* 1974.

Before Aztlán

AZTLÁN CHRONICLES, VOL. 4, NO. 7

For some reason in the mid-sixties I picked up a book *Thus Spake Zarathrustra* a delirous prophetic voice blurred & paradoxical made of labyrinths & lyrics of lava & violet melancholy resentment petals & warm milk a moon milk bitter & deadly & there were the used book stores on Broadway in San Diego where I would cut out with my secret razor knife nude photos & faces & the joke book that I wanted to devour like the joke about the bald man whose head was a third knee old old acrid damp books rusted & stacked *Look* magazines & soiled *Cosmopolitans* & folded *Photoplays* & *National Geographics* where I first saw images of the Holocaust ragged & skull-faced people against wires & walls & smoldering camps & the Nazi "experiments" & then ahhh Toulouse Lautrec's pastels on cardboard the Parisian cabarets the sneaky naughty snickery faces & cool flesh under neon powders & Van Gogh's last painting with a furious sky & crows in exile one day back in S.F. I found Lorca's collected works at the librería nacional in Spanish a burgundy leather volume with images & hand drawings in ink & the poem "Manos Cortadas" I ambled through there in those too serious aisles reading sideways the poetry titles & words like green green verde verde & stood there sat there listened to albums in library booths songs by Baez & Dylan & Josh White & Bach's cantatas & James Brown & the Famous Flames or suddenly took photos of myself in the Greyhound depot the Zen came outta nowhere too the drawings the brushed unfinished circles & the koans those simple little questions with an answer that would take you the rest of your life if you were lucky

NIETZSCHE, ZEN & JAMES BROWN

Circa 1963-1971

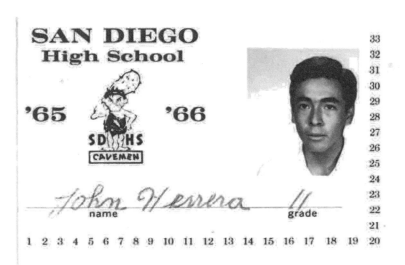

ID card, The Caver. San Diego, California, 1965.

DE TIMBALES Y CASCABELES

¿de donde brota el canto de timbales y
cascabeles?
  El canto más
    fuerte que nuestros jefes derramaron
    sobre las piedras   gruesas de fileros

en los altares   de nuestra tierra santa…
    cuando tus ojos de sol y barro
vean los brazos azules   con venas abiertas
           y
las rodillas quebradas   de nuestros jefes
                       descarnados

sin plumas calurosas de quetzal
                     enterrados

sin flores
  (dentro de las heridas de La Logan)
    ¿oirás
    las lágrimas del jaguar
caer   en tus pómulos?
      ¿sentirás
        la lluvia de gritos locos
        del águila en tu frente?
  ¿de donde brota el calor fibroso
      de nuestra tierra santa?

  ¿caminarás las calles frías grises

perdido

con tu espalda morena cubierta

 con culebras de fierro   ácido

 que chupan   tu corazón?

        El corazón

 de nuestra raza pintado con espejos

 y rayos de bronce

el único corazón   que embriaga

    al jugo del mar

 que embriaga   al pecho de las montañas

  a las llamas rotas en los volcanes

y

     a los vientos

   de las cuatro esquinas

  de nuestra tierra santa

    con cantos de timbales

 y cascabeles…

From *Aztlán Journal*, UCLA, 1971.

LOGAN HEIGHTS &
THE WORLD

For Miguel Estrada, Sammy Vásquez, Mercy Gómez,
Ralph Gómez—Los Beatniks (1958)—& Chris Abani.

I come from a neighborhood
where you can see the Bay from the kitchen.

We kicked the Highway Patrol out
From our varrio and put a Chicano Park
In its place

(right across the street from La Central
where I would buy tortillas and spy
at the tripitas through the butcher's window
noting how they were braided).

Imagine: braids on tripitas?

Would walk home
All the way on National St.
To a gray Victorian house next to a Spanish restaurant
(the only Mexican joint calling itself
Spanish, in the whole area). How do you like that?

El Porvenir, another tortillería, painted
In turquoise, stood out on the corner;
I played with my avocado green top.

Anyway, I lived in apartment #9.
Every now and then I would go out with Jaime
And Miguel Estrada (who knew how to part his hair).
We would kick back at the Coronet theatre
& gawk at the Kool Dude, Pedro Infante
María Antonieta Pons & her Hot Legs
While we spilled the salt and popcorn (5 cents)
On the floor.

One time
I darted out into the street
Making a liquor truck break every bottle
As it slammed on the breaks.

I was chasing Sammy Vásquez, the guy
Who wanted to dance with my girl, Mercedes Gómez,
Because she chose me
And not him as a squaredance partner in fifth grade.

A couple of years later,
The city administration cut a freeway right through
Our varrio. Everything fell apart, vanished.

The little houses with the geraniums singing soprano
And the elastic kids
Grew transparent overnight.

Me and Arnold Nieves, Raymond Sobrantes, Johnny
And Eva Escoto would walk out after school, across
The torn structures and sniff glue
In the condemned apartments.

Everyone lived in a studio set for a B movie
About the coming of Godzilla,
A kind of urban ghost town where
Father Rasura arrived one day
To serve his time at Guadalupe Church.

He showed us films and gave us donuts with chocolate
As we sneered and rattled our fancy code languages

So we went to high school, finally—
The Silent Kids in Mr. Wightman's English class,
A stern and lanky crowd, at lunch time,
Talking about Erich Fromm, Nietszche,

Zen & James Brown and his brand new bag.
We got into choir, sang in Italian, took autoshop
And ran cross-country.

By eleventh grade
We began to grin
Scoping out
The moaning phosphorescent tidal wave coming up
Somewhere near Ocean Beach all the way from Rosarito
And Ensenada.

So, when the Police Dynasty,
The President of the Zoo (an ex–Navy General) and the Mayor
(not to mention the vampire architects) decided
to build a station across from La Central (still standing)
we were ready.

Our little red plastic watch had been ticking
Since we were seven years old, playing marbles &
Spinning tops in the Sector of the Dead.

By '67 the sparking emeralds of the sea
Were in our hands. By '70 we laid some of them down
Forming a circle in the heart of the wasteland;
A simple park, Chicano Park,

A reminder to the world
That we were on the loose.

From *Facegames*, 1987.

Juan Felipe. Los Angeles, circa May 1970. PHOTO BY TOMÁS MENDOZA HARRELL

SOURCES AND COLLECTIONS

Rebozos of Love. Toltecas en Aztlán Publication. Centro Cultural de la Raza, San Diego. 1974.

Exiles of Desire. Lalo Press, Fresno, California, 1983. Reissued by Arte Público Press, University of Houston, 1985.

Facegames. As-Is So & So Publications, Berkeley. 1987.

Akrílica. Alcatraz Editons, Santa Cruz. 1989.

187 Reasons Why Mexicanos Can't Cross the Border. Chapbook, Borderwolf Press, Fresno, California. 1994.

Night Train to Tuxtla. University of Arizona Press, Tucson. 1994.

Mayan Drifter: Chicano Poet in the Lowlands of the Americas. Temple University Press, Pittsburgh. 1997.

Border-Crosser With a Lamborghini Dream. University of Arizona Press, Tucson. 1999.

Notebooks of a Chile Verde Smuggler. University of Arizona Press, Tucson, 2004.

Photography by JFH or part of JFHerrera archives, unless otherwise indicated.

Many gracias, again, to my publishers and editors during the last three decades who published a number of these undocuments before they made their way to this table—bountiful appreciations.

I salute Anthony Cody and Karla R. Garzón-Zárate, former students of mine, for permission to present their work in these pages. And I bow to the folks at em dash, cover designers for City Lights, who poured their molcajete on this Chicano tábula plate, and to the mysterious crew at Gambrinus, book designers who wove la ninota's debut serape.

A drum of soulful laughter for *Johnny Flamingo & Los Hot Plates*— "the One Gig Band," for opening for me at the City Lights book party: Francis "Pancho" Wong on sax, John Carlos Perea on bass, Tom "T-Bone" Lutz, on keyboards, Jimmy "Con Feeling" Biala on skins, and vocalists Genny "La Dervish" Lim, Arlene "Hot Plater Original" Biala, Yoli "SoCal Surfer" Quintana Muñoz and Margarita "The EPT Bombshell" Robles. And cousin Tito Quintana for the Cable Car & the Jazz since 1958. Gracias.